THE FUNDRAISING SERIES

# CORPORATE FUNDRAISING

## Editor Valerie Morton

**Second edition**

D0569225

**The fundraising series**
*Community Fundraising* Harry Brown (editor)
*Corporate Fundraising* Valerie Morton (editor)
*Fundraising Databases* Peter Flory
*Fundraising Strategy* Redmond Mullin
*Legacy Fundraising* Sebastian Wilberforce (editor)
*Trust Fundraising* Anthony Clay (editor)

First edition published 1999 by the Charities Aid Foundation (CAF)

Second edition published 2002 by the Directory of Social Change

Copyright © Directory of Social Change 2002

The material in Appendix One is copyright © Stephen Lloyd 2002

The moral right of the authors has been asserted in accordance
with the Copyrights, Designs and Patents Act 1988.

Published by:
The Directory of Social Change      Tel 020 7209 5151
24 Stephenson Way                   Fax 020 7391 4804
London                              e-mail: books@dsc.org.uk
NW1 2DP                             from whom further copies and a
                                    full publications list are available.

The Directory of Social Change is a Registered Charity no. 800517

Editor Andrew Steeds

Text and cover design Eugenie Dodd Typographics

Typeset by Tradespools Ltd., Frome

Printed and bound by Bell & Bain Ltd., Glasgow

A catalogue record for this book is available from the British Library

ISBN 1 903991 00 5

# Contents

# The fundraising series

Fundraising is a profession in a constant state of evolution; to meet the challenge that this presents, fundraisers must also evolve. Fundraisers look to the future, anticipate need and develop new techniques to fulfil it. The CAF, Institute of Fundraising, DSC fundraising series seeks to address the full range of fundraising activity and technique in one series.

Each successive volume addresses one key element in the full battery of fundraising skills. As the series develops, it will cover the broadest spectrum of fundraising experience currently available. Like fundraising itself, there is no finite limit to the series. As fields develop, so new titles will be added and old ones revised.

The titles are intended not as manuals or directories but as texts explaining and debating fundraising within a framework that derives from the workplace. These texts are to be written as well as used by academics and practitioners alike. Each title addresses the core competencies within the Institute of Fundraising's Certificate of Fundraising Management, ensuring their relevance to working practice.

Each title aims to place the activity covered in the text within its historical, ethical and theoretical context, demonstrating its relationship to current practice. The main body of the text proceeds to analyse current activity and to identify the constituent areas needed to guide future strategy.

The Institute of Fundraising is well situated to assist in the production of this series; without the support, assistance and expertise of its members and their colleagues, the continued development of the series would not be possible. I would like to thank all those who have contributed and are currently contributing to what continues to be the most comprehensive fundraising series available today.

**Andrew Watt**

*Head of policy, Institute of Fundraising*

# About the authors

## Karen Addington

Having graduated with a degree in Modern and Medieval Languages from Cambridge University in 1988, Karen Addington spent some time working in Spain. Following that, she worked for five years in financial services in the City, and studied for professional exams, including law and marketing. She started her career in corporate fundraising with Diabetes UK (then British Diabetic Association) in 1994, with responsibility for developing corporate partnerships with companies in the financial sector. From 1996 to 1998, she worked for NCH as their City fundraising and marketing manager, before returning to Diabetes UK as head of corporate relations.

## Manny Amadi

Manny Amadi is founder and chief executive officer of Cause & Effect, the values-led, applied strategy consultancy specialising in helping organisations to realise their business and societal aspirations through values-driven strategies, programmes and partnerships.

He has worked extensively on corporate social responsibility, organisational purpose and on ground-breaking cause-related marketing campaigns with leading multi-national companies and NGOs.

A key proponent of 'business and society' issues, Manny was designated by the Davos-based World Economic Forum as one of its Global Leaders for Tomorrow and is active on a number of its taskforces. He was awarded an MVO (Member of the Royal Victorian Order) by the Queen, for services to the community.

## Louise Anderson

After eight years working in fundraising and marketing within the voluntary sector, culminating as head of trading and marketing at NCH, Louise Anderson moved within the charity to her current position as project manager within the external affairs division. She now has a remit for capacity building within the fundraising and marketing teams, for building effectiveness within the division and for managing key projects involving high-level corporate sponsors and policy advisors for NCH. She is currently undertaking a part-time Masters in Organisational Psychology to underpin this change in career direction.

## Rachel Billsberry-Grass

Rachel Billsberry-Grass has over ten years' experience in the voluntary sector, which has included regional, events, trusts and corporate fundraising. She has worked for a variety of organisations, including the Muscular Dystrophy Group, the Royal Opera House and Mencap, where she led the corporate fundraising team.

She now works as a freelance fundraising consultant, offering advice and support to a wide range of organisations. In this capacity she has recently been working as head of fundraising for Age Concern England.

## Melanie Burfitt

Melanie Burfitt is head of fundraising at the Lymphoma Association, a national cancer charity helping those affected by lymphatic cancers. She is the Association's first fundraiser, and her fundraising strategy has boosted income to four times its initial level. After starting her working life in marketing, Melanie moved to the voluntary sector in 1988 to join the NSPCC's corporate fundraising department, where she gained many years' experience developing and implementing corporate partnerships. Melanie helped to develop the Institute of Fundraising's first corporate fundraising course, and is now also a trustee of the Triangle Trust 1949 Fund, a grant-giving charitable trust.

## Christopher Carnie

Chris Carnie has been researching wealth and philanthropy since 1990. He was the founder of Factary Europe (www.factary.com) and is the publisher of *Philanthropy in Europe* (www.philanthropyineurope.com), a magazine giving news on private-sector funding in Europe. His first book on prospect research, *Find the Funds – a New Approach to Fundraising Research*, is published by the Directory of Social Change. He is the first researcher to be elected a Fellow of the Institute of Fundraising (1993), and in 1999 was appointed a Fellow of the Royal Society of Arts (RSA). He was Founder Chair of the Institute of Fundraising's Researchers in Fundraising, and is a member of the Association of Professional Researchers for Advancement (USA), a member of the Asociación Profesional de Fundraising (Spain) and of EUconsult.

Chris works with organisations across Europe and the USA, helping them to research and identify wealthy and philanthropic people, foundations and corporations. He consults on research and knowledge management. He writes and trains in research for NGOs and professional bodies, including the International Fund Raising Congress, where he is a regular Master Class leader.

## Tony Elischer

Tony Elischer has over 20 years' hands-on experience in the not-for-profit sector, having worked as head of fundraising for the Imperial Cancer Research Fund and with the Management Centre, the Zoological Society of London and Help the Aged. He has been a consultant for the last six years, working at the highest level across a wide range of causes and organisations, and is the founder of THINK Consulting Solutions, where he is now the managing director.

Tony is an internationally regarded expert on fundraising, having extensive experience of helping charities across the world with strategy, fundraising, management and troubleshooting. He is an accomplished presenter, trainer and writer. He is author of the book *Teach Yourself Fundraising*, has contributed several chapters to other books and written numerous articles, including a monthly column in the magazine *Professional Fundraising*. Internationally, he is on the board of the *Journal of Non-profit and Voluntary Sector Marketing*, the Resource Alliance and is former chair of the International Fundraising Congress. He is a Fellow of the UK's Institute of Fundraising.

## Toby Hester

Toby Hester has spent over 15 years in sponsorship and sports marketing, in the course of which he has worked with brands and companies such as BT, Coca-Cola, Procter & Gamble, and

GlaxoSmithKline. His role at One 2 One (now T-Mobile) has seen him evolve core sponsorship rights in football with the Football Association and Everton FC into a brand-centric cause-related marketing programme that supports football for people with disabilities. One 2 One Ability Counts and sponsorship of the National Association of Disabled Supporters has broken new ground in highlighting the need to provide disabled people with equal opportunities to play and watch football.

## Adrian Hosford

As director of BT's Group Social Policy Team, Adrian Hosford is responsible for co-ordinating BT's combined effort to have as positive an impact on society as possible. This includes BT's community programmes, BT's environmental programme and BT's social responsibility performance (bt.com/betterworld). Previously, Adrian ran BT's Millennium Project, *FutureTalk*, a major BT initiative to help everybody get more from communications in the twenty-first century. Adrian's background is in marketing, where he was the BT brand manager and ran BT's external customer communication programmes worldwide. From ICL, where he was worldwide advertising and direct marketing manager, he joined BT shortly after it was privatised, as part of the new marketing team. Adrian's early career was in the advertising business, working for DMB&B, McCann Erickson and Ketchum.

## Hilary Jacklin

Hilary Jacklin has 14 years' experience of the voluntary sector. She began her career with NSPCC, before moving to the RNIB. There, she was initially corporate fundraising manager, later becoming head of national fundraising. At the turn of the century, she set up her own consultancy and has since worked for a number of organisations, offering a range of services.

## Annabel James

Annabel James joined the NSPCC to lead its corporate fundraising team in 1999, coinciding with the launch of the FULL STOP Campaign: she is responsible for the delivery of a significant proportion of the £250 million appeal target. Before moving to the NSPCC, Annabel spent over ten years working in communications for a number of large consultancies in corporate and financial affairs. In addition to general PR programmes, she worked on community affairs and cause-related marketing initiatives for blue-chip organisations such as Thomas Cook. In addition, Annabel carried out *pro bono* work for a number of charities including the Prince's Trust. Annabel has also worked for Raleigh International, the youth development charity, as head of press and PR.

## Mark Line

Mark Line is director and co-founder of csr network ltd. He has 20 years' experience in corporate environmental management and social responsibility. His areas of expertise include strategy development for large corporations, production of social and environmental reports, and external assurance. His recent clients include BP, Toyota, Agilent and Unilever.

## Stephen Lloyd

Stephen Lloyd is head of the charity department at Bates, Wells & Braithwaite, the leading firm of solicitors for charity law in the United Kingdom. He is also a trustee of five charities, including the Centre for Innovation in Voluntary Action (which he chairs), Blackheath Halls and the Iran Aid Foundation. Stephen writes and lectures extensively on charity law and is author of *The Barclays Guide to Law for Small Business* and *Charities, Trading and the Law*, co-author of *The Charities Act Handbook* and *The Fundraiser's Guide to the Law*, and a contributor to *Jordan's Charities Administration Service*.

Before becoming a solicitor he obtained a degree in History from Bristol University and did voluntary service overseas in Sudan, teaching English.

## Liz Markus

Liz Markus has worked in the UK voluntary sector since 1990, developing sponsorships and events for Oxfam, running corporate Charity-of-the-Year relationships for Imperial Cancer Research Fund and building a team of corporate partnership managers at Crisis. Her work with J Sainsbury's and the *Financial Times* won Institute of Fundraising awards for Best Integrated Corporate Appeal and Best Single Corporate Appeal respectively.

Liz also has experience in commercial marketing, having developed sales promotions and in-store communications for Woolworth's and Pizza Hut when an account handler for the international marketing agency, IMP.

She currently works for THINK Consulting Solutions as the senior consultant in corporate partnerships.

## Valerie Morton

Valerie Morton currently combines a non-executive directorship of Bedfordshire Heartlands Primary Care Trust with working part time for RNIB and as a consultant, offering practical advice and support on a broad range of fundraising and management issues. She is a long-standing and active member of the Institute of Fundraising, supporting a number of their committees and developing and running their corporate fundraising and major donor fundraising training course.

Valerie has been a successful fundraiser for over 23 years. One of the first 'career' fundraisers, she joined Help the Aged after an Economics degree at Durham University and then spent a number of years in schools fundraising before joining NSPCC to develop their employee fundraising initiatives and later to manage the corporate fundraising department. More recent appointments include head of fundraising at the Outward Bound Trust and head of national fundraising at the Royal National Institute for the Blind.

## Adrian Penrose

Adrian Penrose is a communications professional with more than 20 years' experience in lobbying, marketing, campaigning and public relations. Trained as an environmental scientist, Adrian worked for several conservation organisations before joining the RSPB in the run-up to its centenary in 1989. Adrian led corporate fundraising at the RSPB, worked on its Million Members Campaign and became corporate affairs manager. He is a member of the Institute of Public Relations, has been a judge at the IPR (Institute of Public Relations) and other awards and is a trustee of the environmental charity, the World Land Trust. He is now head of communications at the Medical Research Council Centre for Human Nutrition Research.

# Introduction and acknowledgements

Welcome to the second edition of *Corporate Fundraising*, which has been revised and updated to reflect the current environment and to present recent examples of good practice in action.

Looking back over the first edition leads to two conclusions. First, the basic principles of corporate fundraising have stood the test of time, but, second, how much the world has changed!

It is difficult to believe that in a book published only three years ago there was no need to refer to 'corporate social responsibility' (CSR), which is now the context in which many companies, certainly the larger ones, include their support of charities and the community. Chapter 2 provides a very thorough description and analysis of CSR, and Chapter 11, a case study from NSPCC, demonstrates how one charity embraced the CSR issue.

A review of current writing about corporate support of the voluntary sector makes mixed reading. Articles about CSR are frequent, and there are many examples of how companies are taking on board their broad responsibilities to the world in which they operate – yet this is contrasted with a tendency to 'knock' companies for not giving more to charity.

My view is that this tendency to 'name and shame' is unhelpful and highly unlikely to achieve its (presumably) intended objective of increasing levels of giving. As good corporate fundraisers recognise, cash donations are only one element of corporate community support – and a diminishing element at that, as broader, and more creative, win–win partnerships are developed. Many of the published figures do no represent the true level of corporate support. Cash generated for a charity through some form of product promotion is not always classified as a cash donation; it is as likely to be a marketing cost. Gifts in kind are notoriously difficult to value and are often not truly reflected in published figures. A cereal company giving packet space to promoting a healthy-eating message may generate some cash for the charity involved, but what about the benefit to the charity through achievement of an education message? Many companies actively encourage staff fundraising, which must have generated nine-figure sums for charities since it took off as a structured fundraising activity 15 years ago, but much of this will not be captured in formal league tables.

There is a message here for both companies and fundraisers. Companies need to realise that public expectations of them are growing, and to remain competitive they will need to adopt the concept of CSR in its widest form. (Furthermore, if they want to avoid negative criticism, they will need to ensure all forms of activity and support are included in any figures presented.) Corporate fundraisers, and their managers, need to rethink how targets are set. A straight financial target is of course vital, but corporate fundraisers need to recognise their broadening role in achieving a range of objectives for their cause. If a fundraiser for a disability charity, for example, through their contacts with a company, is able to influence that company to employ more disabled staff and to provide better services for disabled customers, that should be recognised as being worth at least as much as a cash donation.

What the growth of CSR has taught us is that corporate fundraising is no longer a discreet way of generating income; it is integral to the achievement of a charity's mission.

## Acknowledgements

This book has been made possible only by the generous support, in time, knowledge and expertise, of the authors and editors involved.

My special thanks go to each of the chapter authors, for providing their own individual insights into the vast and complex subject of corporate fundraising. I am delighted that such experienced and respected fundraisers felt able to support this book and to offer such valuable contributions.

I owe a great debt to the desk editor of this book, Andrew Steeds, whose specialist, and enviable, skills ensured a highly professional publication, and whose good humour enabled me to keep my sanity while facing the challenge of putting the book together.

My thanks go to CAF and the Institute of Fundraising, who had the foresight to conceive this Fundraising series, and to the Directory of

Social Change who entrusted me with producing the revised version
of this book.

## About this book

This book is divided into three broad parts, the first of which provides
a theoretical and practical context to the remaining contributions.
Part 2 uses a number of actual case studies to illustrate many of the
points made in the first section, from the charity's perspective. Part 3
considers corporate–charity partnerships from the company's
perspective, again illustrating the discussion with reference to real
case-study material. Finally, following a concluding chapter, the
Appendices feature an important chapter on the legal and tax issues
surrounding corporate fundraising, an outline structure of a
corporate fundraising strategy, and a directory of useful sources of
information available on the Internet.

**Valerie Morton**

# Background and best practice

# CHAPTER ONE

# Corporate fundraising – a background

**Tony Elischer**

## Corporate support of charities – the roots and origins

The distribution of corporate wealth to charitable endeavour and public benefit mirrors the development of the voluntary sector through history. The United Kingdom is unique in the uninterrupted passage of prosperous trade over many centuries. From the earliest times, there is evidence of both individual and corporate philanthropy based on the fruits of that trade being used to support philanthropic activity.

Mercantile and corporate wealth played a significant part in the development of the physical structures of community and civic life between 1480 and 1660. During this period, corporate benefaction led the way in 'the building of town halls, the provision of corporate plate, endowments to secure the lessening of tax burdens, and a great variety of other gifts designed to make divers communities more attractive and agreeable places in which to work and live.'

In other ways, too, corporate and mercantile wealth, laced with a healthy regard for commercial self-interest, served to promote substantive corporate benefaction and fashion modern society. Even in these early times, the motivation behind corporate support was complex and sophisticated, ranging from pure philanthropic ideal, through ambitious desire for self-promotion and social aggrandisement, to recognition of mutual commercial self-interest.

The presence of local, regional and national corporate support contributed to the success of a wide range of charitable endeavour in the eighteenth and nineteenth centuries. Both in the United Kingdom and also across Europe, wealthy merchants used their own wealth and that of their companies to promote the establishment of a civic and ecumenical infrastructure that the state still regarded as beyond its compass.

As today, London played a leading part. The formation of the City of London around the great livery companies was based on companies' realisation that they would need to provide for more than just individual or corporate wealth if their commercial enterprise was to be maintained and expanded. Throughout subsequent history, City livery companies and the corporate benefaction that supports their work have been hugely influential in the creation of infrastructures, the development of social rehabilitation, and the concerted support for health, education and the alleviation of poverty.

A number of authors have charted the extraordinary impact of the City institutions on the development of philanthropy from the 1600s to the modern era, providing a comprehensive summary of highly sophisticated company giving schemes around the same period. Their findings clearly demonstrate that debate over appropriate levels of corporate philanthropic support as opposed to commercial sponsorship is by no means purely a modern-day phenomenon.

By the late 1800s, there was sufficient public disquiet about the corporate giving policies of these companies to promote a Royal Commission to examine (among other things) the nature of corporate giving programmes, the moral imperative towards philanthropic endeavour that corporate profit demands and the ambiguous nature of philanthropic endeavour when it is inextricably intertwined with commercial benefit. Many of the arguments paraded in the 1880s rehearse the debates over corporate giving that continue to the present day.

## The development of corporate fundraising in the nineteenth century

The origins of what today is classified as corporate fundraising are to be found in the nineteenth century. The abundance of commercial opportunity grounded in the birth of the industrial revolution; commercial advantage, developed through centuries of unrestricted trade; the ease of access to cheap sources of raw material and markets delivered by colonial rule – all conspired to encourage a leap in privately owned corporate wealth at the turn of the nineteenth century. The works and policies of great industrialists of the time, like Cadbury, Wedgwood and Rowntree, pioneered the idea of investing in employees and their local communities.

Much of the force behind this explosion in corporate philanthropy was profoundly personal and often idiosyncratic in nature. The majority of the great reforming corporate institutions were privately owned, family dynasties, themselves highly regimented and controlled through the strict hierarchy of family lineage. Of equal importance was the impact that religious belief played in providing an ideological framework within which corporate philanthropy became an important moral imperative. These great industrial barons were often hard pressed to distinguish between private, family, religious and corporate affiliation. The social and moral condition of employees and their families, the values of the family itself, were intricately intertwined with the fortunes of the company and the advancement of wealth and personal esteem.

There are important lessons for the modern-day corporate fundraiser to take from this complexity, not least in answer to the question, 'Just what is the degree of philanthropic endeavour that might truly be regarded as "corporate" in nature?' Was the development of corporate giving in the Victorian period truly corporate in nature, or was it more importantly grounded in individual philanthropic intent?

# Formalisation of corporate fundraising as an activity

Charity and corporate activity were transformed in the latter part of the twentieth century. Before 1945, both sectors continued to develop organically, working on the long-unbroken, mutually compatible traditions of free trade and corporate beneficence.

There is an inextricable connection between corporate philanthropy and individual giving, because so much individual wealth is the result of commercial success. Much of the product of corporate wealth destined to further philanthropic endeavour was actively channelled into the endowment of large grant-making trusts, or provided by large benefaction to particular service-provision charities that took little active part in soliciting the funds they received.

Some significant proactive corporate fundraising practice did emerge successfully in this period, most notably the development of post-tax employee giving schemes by Barnardo's. In truth, however, the main impetus behind corporate support continued to be vested in the self-enlightened practice of particular employers, as industrialists recognised the value of community support to their business operations and objectives.

From the end of World War II the respective positions of the corporate and charitable sectors have become far more stylised with regard to corporate fundraising. Although privately owned corporate philanthropy remains important in its contribution to corporate fundraising, today it has been matched, if not surpassed, by the post-war growth of publicly owned corporate giving.

As companies have grown larger and more complex, as departmental functionalism within companies provides opportunity for a breadth of competing ideology in the same organisation, as different forms of corporate ownership and structure determine differing corporate outputs, so fundraising success has grown more and more to depend on an understanding of the various motivations behind different types of corporate giving.

The rise of marketing and advertising as pivotal disciplines in corporate enterprise has provided new and potentially lucrative sources of corporate support to the charitable sector. At the same time, they have brought the corporate community itself to a deeper understanding of its own often complex and differing motivations behind various types of support for the charitable sector.

As far as the voluntary sector is concerned, access to new technology, the drive towards corporate public ownership and the development of a more transparent, stakeholder concept of corporate governance has provided it with greater understanding of corporate giving than ever before. Ease of access to this greater knowledge has spurned ever-greater competition for the corporate pound. In turn, this has forced both the corporate and charitable sectors to become more disciplined and professional in the manner in which they address corporate giving.

Today, corporate fundraising has become an essential component in the broader fundraising strategy of the majority of charities. Corporate fundraisers manage their own complex marketing mix and, for their part, major companies have reviewed their support of the charitable sector against far more rigorous benchmarked criteria.

# Understanding corporate fundraising

Fundraisers considering companies as resources need to think in the widest possible terms about the many different ways that companies can support a charity. Companies consist of three basic elements: people, budgets and resources. Fundraisers are used to working with people, as people give to people first; all they need to appreciate is that people in companies are given budgets and resources to achieve set objectives that contribute to the profit of a company. Companies are simply bodies of people combined for commercial purposes to make a profit from a commercial activity. If fundraisers accept this and adopt a positive attitude towards this activity, then they can begin to open their eyes to how they might link into many of the opportunities that companies offer.

Figure 1 seeks to define a typical range of people, budgets and resources that might be found in a company and to list a typical range of benefits that a charity might offer a company. Too many charities limit their approaches by thinking simply of the chair, marketing director and the charity committee. Yet there are many more access points and potential areas from which to generate support.

The focus is all too often on money, rather than thinking through the full spectrum of charitable giving: time, money and goods. As this area becomes more competitive, it is essential to think more creatively and to find more unique ways of working with companies. It is also necessary to think about a relationship and how to start and develop it rather than always aspiring to the top and the highest value forms of support.

**FIGURE 1** HOW THE PEOPLE IN A COMPANY MAY BENEFIT A CHARITY

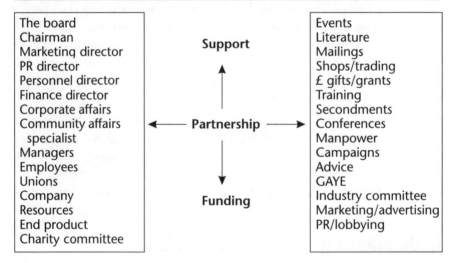

© AMC Elischer

## The key players in a company

At the top of most companies is the **board**, the body of people who represent the shareholders' interests and generally serve to keep the company on track and operating at an acceptable profit level.

This group is often a considerable size with people drawn from all walks of life, many of whom may already be known to a charity through the contacts of its trustees and board. The value of these contacts is their ability to advise, guide and facilitate introductions to different staff and departments within their company. Many directors also serve on more than one board, so cultivation is the key in this area.

Under the board is the **chair**, **chief executive** or **managing director** (depending on the size and organisational format of the company), the key person who leads and guides the company. As the most powerful person, they are well targeted by charities for support of varying kinds, and many of them have developed sophisticated defence shields as a result.

Historically, this person was seen as the key to philanthropic funds and general influence within the company. Now, although the influence remains, in many cases the funds have been allocated to specialists or to other budgets where corporate objectives can be achieved through their deployment. As in the case of the board, the main gift this person can give is their interest in and endorsement of your cause, leading to advice and guidance on how to work with companies in general.

Of the directors that are responsible to the chair, and who represent the key functions within a company, **marketing** has to be the top prospect. Charities appear to think that marketing directors have lots of money, which they do, but for very tightly defined purposes. The starting place here must be to understand that marketing is 'the process responsible for identifying, satisfying and anticipating customer requirements profitably'. Marketing is the heart of a company, and any charity that chooses to target it with a proposition or request should ask itself how that proposition is helping to fulfil marketing's role for the company. This is the commercial end of seeking corporate support, where sponsorship and cause-related marketing are key. As other chapters will illustrate, the rewards are high, but so are the levels of competition and the technical skill required to work effectively in this area.

Charities invest considerable resources in targeting marketing departments for sales promotions or cause-related marketing opportunities. In general, these approaches are unsuccessful. Companies will decide themselves when these types of activities are appropriate and they will then seek suitable partners. Charities aiming to be successful in this area should concentrate on building a reputation for working effectively with companies and on developing their brand awareness in the market place. This way they will find themselves on company shortlists for opportunities. Only an exceptional idea will truly succeed from cold in this area; to introduce ideas and achieve a hearing, existing relationships are the key.

## The main departments

**Public relations** (PR) is a useful point of contact for charities for several reasons, most obviously because this department acts as the interface between a company and the public and may therefore be a good place for information, views and guidance.

Until the advent of payroll giving, no one really paid much attention to the **personnel**, or **human resources** (HR) department, and they were relatively easy to gain access to and befriend. This is no longer necessarily the case, as charities are seen to be after one thing only: access to employees to promote payroll schemes. Charities need to exercise lateral thinking in this important area, as HR is a real key to company networks and employees.

HR departments purchase and plan training for employees. Many of these training places go to waste each year through sickness and changes in plans. A charity registering an interest in such opportunities can often be contacted at short notice and offered places on sales, presentation or management courses for its staff or volunteers. Indeed, some companies now run extra courses just to offer to the voluntary sector. Volunteering and secondment are two further areas for consideration here.

**Corporate affairs** is often the silent function within major companies, the role of which can vary from handling relationships with government, to co-ordinating planning, to defining and protecting the company image or brand, or even preparing crisis PR strategies. Any of these areas is at a high level of operation that usually involves reporting to the chair and certainly plays a major role in guiding the company and its activities.

Finance, sales and other directors in a company, and their functions, can be analysed in this way, but the key point is that each position and function within a company has the potential to offer opportunities. It is a matter of thinking outside conventional wisdom to find an appropriate approach that may help a charity stand out from the crowd.

One other area worth noting in relation to the key people and functions is any **specialist functions** a company may have that could either have a particular affinity with your cause or be of specialist interest. For example, charities working in medical research may find a link with company medical officers a useful way into a company, and charities for children may find links with crèche managers appropriate. Legal officers, economists or IT specialists may offer specific skills to charities at a particular stage of their development.

## Employees, resources and other agencies

Under these main functions you have an army of **employees** who all offer the potential to introduce a charity to the workplace and to their company. Too few charities take the trouble to introduce corporate fundraising to their donors and volunteers through newsletters and mailings. Simply highlighting the value of the area and asking for contacts or interest in helping to develop programmes may provide useful leads. Companies are devolving more power and decisions to employees, particularly in the area of charity and community involvement. Charities need to respond to this by working both at head-office and at grassroots level.

Beyond people there are **resources**, a major area of opportunity often overlooked in the UK, or certainly seen as a secondary option for support. Yet this is an area where it is often easier to get a gift, and for the company to give, since a gift of resources does not necessarily mean money off the bottom line. A brainstorm around this area will lead to many different options:

- gift of end-product for use, resale or as a prize
- use of empty buildings for office space
- use of corporate buildings for meetings or events
- photocopying and printing facilities
- stationery supplies
- old office equipment: furniture, computers, etc.

As in the USA, there are now specialist UK charities that encourage these gifts, promote their value and act as a clearing-house for companies who want to find recipients. A well thought-out programme will bring the benefit of another way of linking with companies.

Any review of companies would not be complete without highlighting the many **auxiliary agencies** that companies are increasingly using to fulfil specific roles: advertising, PR, sponsorship, recruitment, sales promotion, etc. These agencies offer another way into companies; more importantly, they offer a filter for ideas. Many of these agencies are retained to solve problems, create opportunities and basically to have good ideas on behalf of the company.

Befriending them can provide an invaluable opportunity to 'test' your ideas and to seek guidance on refinement and more appropriate targeting. Charities should also strive to achieve awareness of their organisation, its activities and interest in working with the corporate sector through this group.

At the base of the 'company as a resource' model is the traditional **charity committee**, which will distribute the donations budget that many companies still have. The demands on these funds inevitably mean that exceptional skills are needed if a case is to succeed. A charity must also be prepared to accept the 'lottery' element of the distribution of these funds. Despite this, it is almost essential that charities approach these committees if they are to build profile and to seek funding in return for minimal requirements. As with PR, charity committees can be a friend to the charity sector, offering guidance and advice, but charities should be clear about their strategy before making approaches and recognise that the creative approaches required to gain access to marketing budgets do not necessarily apply here.

This account of the typical people, budgets and resources to be found within companies demonstrates the wide range of opportunities available and illustrates why every charity should have corporate support in their funding portfolio. The secret is to set a strategy and to attempt a different approach from that made by the other 180,000 charities that have targeted companies as a potentially wealthy source of donations.

This model applies in full only to larger companies, although many of the ideas and elements will still apply to medium-sized, regionally based companies. Research will indicate which companies follow this model and where you need to make suitable adjustments to the model and its thinking. Rather than starting with national companies – which is what everyone tends to do – it would be easier to start with the hundreds of thousands of local and regional companies that rarely receive imaginative professional approaches for their support.

The right hand side of Figure 1 illustrates some of the needs and opportunities a typical charity may have in relation to companies. Each charity needs to lay out its own 'market stall' before approaching companies, in order to draw up a priority and take a flexible approach when seeking partnerships with companies. Cold approaches are becoming increasingly difficult, especially when the first approach is for money. Charities need to consider how they can start a dialogue and how to build it over time, as confidence and credibility build.

# The overall perspective

In recent years corporate fundraising has undergone a shift in emphasis. There has been a move away from the technique whereby specific roles were allocated in corporate fundraising teams to a more generalist function with a limited client portfolio. Figure 2 illustrates this structure and highlights the importance of the individual, who is at the centre and must possess an understanding and overview of all the components.

**FIGURE 2** THE FIVE ELEMENTS OF CORPORATE FUNDRAISING

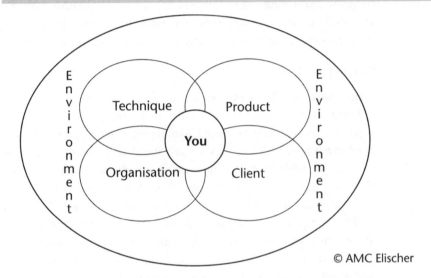

© AMC Elischer

The five elements identified within the environment are the headings under which all elements of the corporate fundraising process fit. The division within this model helps to group and analyse all the elements; it also serves to highlight the variables in this activity that the fundraiser controls.

## You

The individual is the driving force behind any fundraising. You need to understand and appreciate how the corporate sector works and, from these core skills, to review your attitude towards your product and the task of selling it to companies. It is the job of the corporate fundraiser to identify projects within their organisation that have the potential to attract the different forms of corporate support, and then to package them in the appropriate way. This process is an integral part of developing belief and ownership in the fundraiser. In commercial selling, 'the first sale we have to make is to ourselves'. It is hard to convey enthusiasm, particularly through the written word, but belief comes through time and time again.

Corporate fundraising is high-energy fundraising and fiercely competitive. In addition to the unique selling propositions (USPs) of the project and the charity, energy, belief and commitment can play a major part – after all, people 'give to people first, whatever else second'. Many charities exclude corporate opportunities because they believe that they have an unpopular cause that lacks 'sex appeal'; such charities are disadvantaging themselves before they start. Virtually every charitable cause can gain some sort of corporate support, providing the fundraiser has a positive mental attitude. Corporate fundraising demands dedication, passion and commitment, arguably beyond any other fundraising technique.

## Product

Many charities still operate with a piecemeal set of projects, often inflicted on the corporate fundraiser as the things for which other departments and people would like funding or support. You will need to organise a thorough audit of your charity and develop a full portfolio of projects that form your core products in the market place if you are to succeed. People often do not realise the dual battles corporate fundraisers must face in not only marketing their portfolios, but also establishing them in the first place. This technique often involves 'selling' the name of the organisation and aligning its values with those of a commercial company, so it is important to gain approval and commitment at all levels of a charity. Think of your corporate fundraising department or activity as a shop that needs stocking with products attractive to consumers. Like a shop you should try new products but, just as importantly, you should not take up valuable shelf space stocking products that clearly are not going to sell.

Try to identify projects that help companies to 'reach the unreachable'; profile your audiences; think creatively around the people of influence to whom you have access, and develop a list of celebrity supporters.

As consumers we expect quality and service in our transactions with companies, yet in the corporate fundraising area we do not do enough to ensure that the same attributes apply to our activities. Consider every aspect of your product and the way you market and deliver it; strive for the highest level of quality, and refuse to settle for second best, just because you are a charity. People's expectations of service increase each year, and more and more companies fail to deliver in this area; for their own reputation and survival, and that of the sector as a whole, charities have to deliver.

## Technique

There are many and varied techniques within corporate fundraising, at the core of which there are a number of essential techniques that charities wishing to exploit and explore the potential of corporate support must master. The challenge for fundraisers is to extend, develop and refine these techniques to make them offer more for both the charity and the company. The key elements of sponsorship do not vary, but success depends on how people translate and use these elements. The textbook and training course are vital to understanding, but adapting and learning from experience are more important. Success with techniques means not being hung up about them, viewing them as instruments to be used rather than rules to be obeyed.

The key skill in all areas of corporate fundraising is the ability to put yourself in the place of the person you are approaching, to get into their mind and circumstances. Experience and awareness provide the ability to identify the correct motivator to use. What is the trigger to get the contact in the company to say 'Yes'? Motivators are governed by the mind and the heart: the mind reviews the logic, business benefits and general appropriateness; the heart reviews the cause, its need and emotional appeal.

The foundations of a good approach are built upon research, but applying imagination and creativity to a technique are two other 'converters' that will distinguish your approach from others. Capturing your prospect's imagination is an important part of your approach.

## Client

Most people will have experienced the courting process. Corporate fundraisers should use this experience and begin to view their approaches to companies as individual courting experiences. They should see these approaches in terms of building relationships, promoting understanding and mutual respect, and agreeing to partnerships where both parties are comfortable and content with their part of the agreement – all in the recognition that different relationships require different timings, approaches and energy levels.

There is an old adage that it is ten times more difficult to acquire a new client than it is to retain and upgrade an existing one, and yet the drive of much corporate activity is to acquire new clients to meet the needs of new projects. Why? Just like a consumer purchasing any item, if clients are happy with the product and service they receive they are likely to return for more, or at least to be receptive to further approaches and propositions. This highlights the need to build a true partnership to enable you to look on clients as a return on your investment. By making past corporate partners friends of the charity, there is not only a greater possibility of further joint projects but also the opportunity to ask for introductions and recommendations to other key prospects you have identified.

### Organisation

Organisation is the area most frequently neglected by the corporate fundraiser. The corporate fundraising mix is so wide that most organisations will find a technique that is right for them and their available resources. The key word is resources: a corporate fundraiser must define precisely what investment the organisation is prepared to commit to this area, since this will influence their choice of technique as much as the work of the organisation.

The ethical issues surrounding corporate fundraising should be reviewed under this heading. These issues will vary for each organisation, and it is important to set a policy that is right for the individual needs of the organisation: are there areas of commerce and industry with which the organisation does not feel compatible or with which it would not feel comfortable aligning itself? The important thing is to agree the policy before any corporate approaches or negotiations are instigated.

## Corporate alertness

Any corporate fundraising function should promote 'corporate alertness' within their organisation and encourage staff to pick up on any corporate contact made by either the company or anyone associated with the charity, from trustees to directors to volunteers and donors. Organisations often miss the contacts that are under their noses; make sure every part of the organisation is aware of the importance of companies and any contacts that exist with them.

The model presented in Figure 2 should be used as a flexible framework to encourage fundraisers in the corporate area to consider the principal component parts that will lead to success. New ideas, experience and environment changes should be integrated into the circles as they occur, making it an ever-evolving structure for fundraising development and achievement.

# CHAPTER TWO

# Corporate fundraising in context – corporate social responsibility

**Mark Line**

## What is corporate social responsibility?

There is increasing pressure today on companies not just to share their wealth with society through sponsorship and donations but also to demonstrate that their core business activities at best are a benefit to society and at worst pose no threat to society. At the heart of the corporate–charity relationship is the issue of corporate social responsibility (CSR).

CSR is interpreted in many different ways, and there is as yet no universally agreed definition. It is often described as a three-pillar structure supported by the core issues: environment, society and economics. As a concept, CSR is about a holistic and sustainable approach to business that considers all its potential impacts and responsibilities to society, the environment and shareholders, rather than focusing solely on financial responsibilities to shareholders, as has traditionally been the case.

For a company to take account of all its impacts on society and the environment, it must first understand what these impacts might be. The key to this is engagement with stakeholders – both within the organisation and outside in society. Transparency and engagement are the tools by which a company can build a relationship with the world outside, but they are equally important within the organisation in managing employee expectations and demands.

Within the social agenda, issues such as human rights, equal opportunities, and work–life balance are key. At present, environmental stewardship is more established and better developed than social accountability and has a more clearly defined management approach. The ambiguity surrounding the social element of CSR has led some to interpret it as corporate philanthropy. In some cases it has been seen as an add-on with no real links to core business activities, rather than as an integral part of managing the business.

# The history of CSR

Financial performance has always been the primary focus for business. Profits have traditionally indicated a company's level of success. In the 1970s the environmental movement started to promote green issues, and by the 1980s some large companies were beginning to think about the environmental impact of their business and had developed environmental reporting and management systems: for example, the environmental report IBM produced in 2000 was the eleventh of its kind.[1] However, despite this emergence of environmental issues, and the way they were linked to health and safety, it took several significant events to act as catalysts for pushing the CSR agenda and positive engagement forward at the corporate level.

Over the last 20 years, several key incidents have acted as wake-up calls to multinational companies and forced them to take a closer look at their business and the CSR agenda. On the international front, Union Carbide, a US chemical company, experienced the first major environmental and human safety disaster involving both employees and local communities at its pesticide plant in Bhopal, northern India. In 1984 the plant leaked 40 tonnes of toxic gases, killing between 2,000 and 8,000 people. The accident sparked a vicious debate about companies' double standards, and the fact that they paid less attention to the environment and safety in developing countries than they did at home. Closer to home, Shell International was flung to the forefront of public attention in 1994 over its involvement in Nigeria. Just a year later it was under scrutiny again when it tried to dump the Brent Spar platform in the North Sea. The public outcry and criticism these events received had not been experienced by a leading multinational corporation before, and they left not just Shell but all multinationals reeling from the shock. Almost ten years later these incidents are still cited as a turning point in the advance of corporate social accountability.

Most recently, the clothing company Nike and the oil giant Exxon-Mobil have faced public criticism over their attitudes to child labour and climate change. Mounting pressure from both the general public and, increasingly, also from shareholders has forced many companies to reflect upon their responsibilities.

Over the last decade, companies have faced new incentives to act responsibly in the shape of shareholder pressure, not just from the

---

[1] The 2001 Benchmark Survey of The State of Global Environmental and Social Reporting, csr network ltd, 2001.

general public, but also in a significant rise in 'socially responsible or ethical investment' (SRI). According to the new UK index for SRI, *FTSE 4 Good* (July 2001), there are more than 50 retail ethical funds in the UK alone and the value of these funds grew from £199.3 million in 1989 to £3.7 billion in 2000, an increase of over 1,750 per cent.

Although the business case for adopting CSR strategies is so far based primarily on reputational benefit, research shows that returns from ethical stocks are at least comparable with those for more traditional equity investment. With individuals requesting that their investments be 'ethical' and the UK government introducing the new requirement for pension funds to state in their investment policies the extent to which they take account of ethical, social, and environmental issues, companies are beginning to sit up and take note.

# Current initiatives

The three elements of CSR that make up the 'triple bottom line' are at varying stages of development. Economic management systems and financial reporting have been well established for many years, while management systems and reporting indicators for environmental stewardship are only now becoming standardised. One example is the ISO 14001 standard, now widely recognised and respected as an environmental management tool. However, the social aspect of CSR has yet to be defined and reporting indicators agreed on. In addition, the integration of all three elements into a comprehensive business approach is still being hotly debated. In an attempt to develop practical tools that might achieve these aims, a number of initiatives have emerged around the key aspects of reporting, social accounting, and sustainable development guidelines. These initiatives are not legally binding but rely on the voluntary participation of companies for their success.

# Guidelines

Over the last ten years a large number of guidelines, principles and codes have emerged relating to CSR. Many of these have been developed by independent organisations and international forums set up specifically for that purpose; others have been put together by companies that are trying to determine what CSR means for them. Of all these various types of guidelines, we have chosen to highlight three, which are among the more established and better known.

As early as 1976, the member governments of the Organisation for Economic Co-operation and Development (OECD) adopted the OECD Declaration on International Investment and Multinational Enterprises, one part of which is the Guidelines for Multinational Enterprises. The guidelines are recommendations promoted by the 30 member governments for multinational enterprises (MNEs) operating in or from their country. The unique characteristic of these guidelines is that they are the only comprehensive, multilaterally endorsed code of conduct for MNEs in the world. The voluntary guidelines seek to encourage better understanding and co-operation between MNEs and the countries in which they operate. To this end, they are supported and at times revised by business and labour organisations, non-governmental organisations and the member governments. In 2000, the guidelines were reviewed to take into consideration the evolution of business practices and the CSR agenda.

In 1977, the Reverend Leon Sullivan initiated the Sullivan Principles, which was then a code of conduct for companies operating in South Africa. These principles are acknowledged to be one of the most effective efforts to end discrimination in the workplace in the Republic of South Africa, and they became a major platform on which others could speak out for equal rights and against the apartheid system. Today the Sullivan Principles encourage companies and organisations, large or small, all over the world to achieve greater economic, social and political justice. Any type of organisation may sign up to these principles regardless of its origin. The eight .principles cover respect for universal human rights, equal opportunities, freedom of association, development of economic and social opportunities for employees, protection of the environment, promotion of sustainable development, combating corruption and bribery, community involvement, and promotion of fair trade. Each organisation that signs up to the principles must submit an annual account that demonstrates the steps they have taken to live up to their commitment. To date, almost 200 private-sector companies have endorsed the principles as well as an additional 25 not-for-profit and government-based organisations. In many countries, adoption of such principles is being used as an indicator of a company's commitment to CSR.

More recently, in 2000, the United Nations launched its Global Compact. The UN Global Compact is a set of nine principles based on existing international conventions such as the Universal Declaration of Human Rights, the International Labour Organisation's Fundamental Principles on Rights at Work, and the Rio Principles on Environment and Development. The principles cover the three areas of human rights, labour and environment. The Global Compact was drawn up in response to a challenge to world business leaders by UN Secretary General Kofi Annan to help build a more sustainable global economy that benefits all the world's people. Several hundred companies have already signed up to the Global Compact and are implementing the nine principles in their business.

## Social accounting

Transparency, accountability and stakeholder engagement are the buzzwords that describe the key components of any CSR strategy. A number of initiatives have been set up to develop frameworks to formalise these concepts and turn them into processes that can become practical tools for CSR management.

In 1999/2000, the Institute of Social and Ethical Accountability (ISEA) developed its AA1000 framework with such an aim in mind. AA1000 is a management tool that focuses particularly on transparency through ethical accounting, auditing and reporting. A year later ISEA is now developing AA10005, and hopes to take the tool a step further with the focus shifted to learning and change through stakeholder interaction.

In a similar way, Project Sigma aims to promote an integrated approach to sustainability in business. In its first phase, Sigma sought to identify all the existing sustainability and CSR standards and tools with a view to creating an overarching framework that would bring all the various initiatives together.

SA8000 is a set of social accountability standards against which companies can be audited. The standard covers issues such as child labour, forced labour, health and safety, freedom of association, and discrimination, and has been widely used by companies with operations in countries where these issues are especially relevant. Achieving certification against the standard is seen by many as a useful means of displaying their commitment to social accountability and CSR.

## Reporting

Environmental and social reporting is key to stakeholder engagement, but here again there are many ways of reporting. How and what to report are still big questions.

The Global Reporting Initiative (GRI) set up in 1997 is in the process of developing its Sustainability Reporting Guidelines (June 2001), a framework for combined economic, environmental and social reporting. Their aim is to develop a mechanism that effectively conveys information to all interested parties and resolves the increasingly confrontational and antagonistic relationship that many companies experience with sections of civil society. As the guidelines state, 'as diverse groups seek information, business encounters escalating demands in queries that are inconsistent, giving rise to even more confusion and frustration. The GRI is an attempt to resolve this paradox.'

So what has been the effect of the GRI guidelines on the CSR agenda? During 2000/2001, the GRI piloted its first draft of guidelines, which over 60 companies are already following in their reporting. One of the pilot companies, General Motors Corporation, commented:

*Although the GRI has come a long way since its genesis, its long-term objectives will be achieved only by the continued focus, co-operation, and support of an ever-broadening constituency of stakeholders. But the opportunity is significant – to create a new, global model for disclosure and accountability that is more relevant to the needs and interests of all stakeholders.*[2]

The GRI is not a prescriptive 'recipe' for the structure of a report. Companies have been able to reflect the common elements of reporting as set out in the guidelines, without losing the necessary individuality and focus of their reports. The guidelines are now seen by many as an effective mechanism for achieving the transparency required by stakeholders:

*The transparency of GRI has helped us immeasurably at Ford ... It was absolutely necessary and right for us to adopt GRI. We're glad we did.* (John Rintamaki, Group Vice President and Chief of Staff, Ford Motor Company, November 2000)[3]

On a simple level, the guidelines suggest a series of 'general' and 'organisation-specific' indicators of performance; however, the question of what to report remains a dilemma for many companies. At the extreme, some would say that the stakeholders of a company should have a strong influence on what should be reported. However, each stakeholder group will have different priorities, and mapping these out can in itself be an exercise that

---

[2] Judith Mullins, General Motors Corporation, 'Environmental, Health and Safety Auditing' roundtable newsletter, February 2000
[3] Source: www.globalreporting.org

yields valuable intelligence about how the company is perceived. Figure 3 shows an example of how the 'footprint' of an organisation can be 'mapped' as a first step towards determining what measures and indicators should be reported.

# The fundraising context

It is in this context of increasing environmental and social account-ability that corporate fundraising now finds itself. Today fundraisers and donors are looking for a working partnership that provides mutual benefit not only in terms of funds but also, and often equally importantly, in terms of publicity and reputation. Companies and charities alike are careful to choose fundraising partners that are likely to reflect well on their own operations. Fundraising is not about raising funds in whatever way possible; it is about using the partnership to develop a common approach. For charities this means ensuring that their corporate partner is doing the right thing in terms of CSR and that they are not at risk of becoming embroiled in scandal and misconduct. For the company one aspect of corpor-ate giving is selecting causes that fulfil the company policies on CSR or sustainable development and promote the industry sector in which they operate.

A large number of companies now have their own charitable foun-dations registered as charities from which they conduct their social investment programmes, donating both time and funds. In most cases the work of the foundation complements the attitudes and policies of the parent company. One of the programmes of the Shell Foundation, which was established in 1999, is the Sustainable Energy Programme. SEP supports not-for-profit projects all over the world that are developing and researching sustainable energy solu-tions and consumption.

As well as choosing causes that complement and further their busi-ness activities, companies use charities in cause-related marketing. Cause-related marketing may be defined (as Business in the Com-munity does) as a commercial activity by which businesses and charities or causes form a partnership with each other for mutual benefit. Research by Business in the Community has found that con-sumers increasingly expect companies to involve themselves in the local community: 81 per cent of consumers agree that they are more likely to buy a product or service that is associated with a cause they care about, price and quality being equal; 75 per cent of chief executives, marketing directors and community affairs

# FIGURE 3 MAPPING THE FOOTPRINT[4]

Stakeholders

| CSR key issues | Directors/ shareholders/ investors | Employees | Customers | Business partners | Suppliers | Regulators | NGOs/ pressure groups | Local communities | Wider society |
|---|---|---|---|---|---|---|---|---|---|
| Values and governance | High | Low | Low | Medium | Low | Medium | Low | Low | Low |
| Regulations | Low | Low | Low | Medium | Low | High | Low | Medium | Low |
| Business operations | Low | Medium | High | High | Medium | Medium | High | Low | Low |
| Accountability | Low | High | Medium | Low | Low | Medium | Low | Low | Low |
| Human rights | Low | High | Medium | Low | High | High | High | Low | Medium |
| Employee rights | Low | High | Low | Medium | High | High | High | Low | Low |
| Business context | High | Medium | Low | Medium | Low | Low | Low | Low | Low |
| Product impact | Low | Low | High | Medium | Low | Medium | Medium | Medium | Medium |
| Social investment | Low | Low | Low | Low | Low | Low | Medium | High | Medium |
| Impact on other species | Low | Low | Low | Low | Low | Medium | Medium | Medium | High |
| Impact on environment | Medium | Medium | Medium | Medium | High | High | High | High | High |
| Health and safety | Low | High | Medium | Medium | High | High | High | High | High |

Key
- ■ High interest/many relevant issues
- ▨ Medium interest/some relevant issues
- □ Low interest/few relevant issues

directors believe that cause-related marketing can enhance corporate or brand reputation.

In a world where consumers and stakeholders are making ever-more vociferous demands of today's business community, companies are having to reassess not only their involvement in the local community but also the core values that drive their business. Charities are keen to team up, but not at any price.

## Useful web sites

**www.accountability.org.uk** – Institute of Social and Ethical AccountAbility

**www.bitc.org.uk** – Business in the Community

**www.projectsigma.com** – The Sigma Project

**www.cepaa.org** – Social Accountability International – SA8000

**www.europa.eu.int** – European Union

**www.ftse4good.co.uk** – FTSE4Good

**www.globalreporting.org** – Global Reporting Initiative

---

[4] Adapted from *Corporate Social Responsibility – Making Good Business Sense* WBCSD January 2000

**www.globalsullivanprinciples.org** – Global Sullivan Principles

**www.oecd.org** – Organisation for Economic Co-operation and Development

**www.shellfoundation.org** – The Shell Foundation

**www.unglobalcompact.org** – United Nations Global Compact

# CHAPTER THREE

# Managing corporate fundraising
### Melanie Burfitt

# Introduction

Companies' support of charities and the community – often known as corporate community involvement (CCI) – is today more formal and more commercial than it used to be. It is a big business: according to a *Corporate Citizen* survey, UK-based companies spent more than £544 million on community contributions in the UK and across the world in 1999/2000.

Alliances between companies and charities should be two-way relationships. The essence of the activity is partnership, and the charity that can help a company most fully meet its objectives is the one most likely to receive its support. Similarly the charity should ensure that its own objectives are articulated, pursued and evaluated throughout the course of the partnership.

The management of such relationships requires specialist skills. Charities not only need a crack sales team to open the door and win the business; they also require skilled account managers to manage and nurture projects, and to recognise and develop the full potential of relationships.

In medium-sized to larger charities, such fundraising is likely to be the responsibility of a corporate fundraising section, which may have anything from one to thirty staff. In a smaller charity, this function may be integrated into the responsibilities of the sole fundraiser or the chief executive.

Either way, particular attention needs to be paid to the way in which a charity approaches, negotiates with and manages partnerships with a commercial company; this chapter provides some indication of how to organise that activity.

# The role and scope of corporate fundraising

## What is corporate fundraising, and how does it work?

Companies can support charities in a variety of ways, some of which give the company measurable commercial benefits. It is common practice for companies to seek partnerships that offer tangible benefits to themselves – such as publicity, enhanced image, goodwill with staff, customers and suppliers – as well as providing funds and awareness for the charity.

Chapter 1 explained in detail the role of the company as a resource. Broadly speaking, this role may be characterised as four different ways in which companies may provide support to charities.

### 1 Philanthropic giving

Some companies still continue the time-honoured tradition of disinterested philanthropy and give donations to charities with 'no strings attached'; some have corporate trusts or foundations specifically set up as a means of providing community support efficiently and tax-effectively.

In the current climate, where commercial partnerships between companies and charities are increasingly high profile, the 'Chairman's wife's influence' is less and less evident. However, this can still be an important and potentially valuable route to support, and should not be overlooked.

Instead of making a number of smaller donations to a variety of charities on demand, many companies now have an agreed and finite budget to distribute in order to make more impact. Policies may support the company's corporate strategy. Royal Mail (formerly Consignia), for example, has focused its support in line with its business: its £250,000 Stepping Stone Fund supports community groups and charities working to improve adult literacy.

In addition, the whole staff, rather than management alone, now very often play an active role in the distribution of donations, either through recommendations or through representation on the charity committee.

Fundraisers in search of corporate donations are advised to make a targeted approach to companies rather than employing large-scale mailshots.

## 2 Cause-related marketing (CRM)

A company may use its marketing budget for a promotion or a sponsorship linked to a cause. Linking a company's name to a well-respected charity can be a powerful marketing technique. The key criterion for such activity is that it meets the company's marketing objectives, which may be launching a new product or service, or increasing the uptake of such products or services.

Cause-related marketing (CRM) is becoming more and more a part of a company's overall business strategy, rather than an ad-hoc marketing activity. Companies undertaking CRM will also be seeking a return on their investment: their objective is to take advantage of the charity's positive image in order to enhance their own image, create goodwill, and build loyalty with their customers. For a cause-related activity to achieve maximum success, there needs to be synergy between the company and the charity, either because the product area is relevant or because there is a shared target audience.

CRM can raise substantial funds for charities, but it tends to be only charities with a high, and clearly defined, profile that are approached by companies. Charities need to be aware that CRM, and charity promotions in particular, is a specialist area, and the legality of ideas should be carefully checked by an expert. Pro-actively targeting companies for joint promotions can be very labour intensive; for this reason, many charities are reactive rather than proactive in this area of fundraising (see Chapter 5 for a more detailed analysis of CRM).

## 3 Employee support

The third potential source of income from a company is through its employees. This may involve companies adopting a particular cause as their Charity of the Year (as Tesco, for example, adopted Cystic Fibrosis Trust in 2002). An adoption can be for a shorter period of time than this, or indeed may be a long-term partnership. (Children's or cancer charities appear to be the most motivational areas for staff fundraising: of *Corporate Citizen's* top ten staff fundraising charities for 1999/2000 all except one, Shelter, belong in these categories.)

A fundraising challenge is issued to staff, with money raised often being matched by the company, in part or in full, and corporate events scheduled throughout the adoption period to raise additional funds.

A formal adoption can be a major opportunity for a charity with the resources and staff to take advantage of it. For the company, such an activity can boost staff morale, and encourage team building and the development of staff skills. It can generate useful publicity, particularly locally, give the company a higher profile within the community, and help recruit and retain staff and develop skills.

It is, however, important to note that being chosen as a Charity of the Year will cause a sudden increase in annual income for the adopted charity which it will not necessarily be possible to sustain in subsequent years, and will require extensive resources – often financial as well as staff.

Fundraising within a company is sometimes carried out less formally by a core group of active fundraisers, operating often on an ad-hoc basis but sometimes as a formal committee. Identifying and building a relationship with these people can be an excellent way into a company, particularly for smaller charities or those with less popular causes. Charities with members or clients should also look at the possibility of asking these people to help open doors into companies.

Funds can also be raised from employees through Give As You Earn, which allows staff to make regular, tax-efficient donations to their choice of charities through deductions from their pay, and has the benefit, until April 2003, of being boosted by a 10 per cent bonus from government.

A growing area of employee support is through volunteering. Although some charities put this much lower down the pecking order than monetary support, employee volunteering can often be of equal, or greater, value to charities, and may be worth serious consideration.

## 4 Transferring resources

Another source of return to charities from companies involves the transfer of resources (gifts in kind) or the temporary transfer of staff (secondment). A company may find it more cost effective to give its own products (or equipment that is no longer needed) than a cash donation: for example, Dixons recently donated gift vouchers to the Lymphoma Association for a digital camera.

Gifts in kind and secondments can not only be very valuable to charities in their own right but can also open the door to future, more profitable, partnerships. A number of charities exploit the potential of gifts in kind, with the Prince's Trust and Crisis topping the league with over £2 million worth of donated goods and services each.[1]

# The management of corporate fundraising

## Human resources

A good corporate fundraiser requires specialist skills: as a result, experienced staff are often in short supply. The fundraiser needs to be an individual who is credible at senior corporate level, commercially aware and an excellent communicator. This individual will need to be an ambassador for the cause as well as the internal champion of the benefits of corporate partnerships within his or her charity. Two skills that are crucial, but often overlooked, are innovation and creativity.

Most charities involved in corporate fundraising now have an account management structure like that used in advertising agencies, with each team member responsible for a number of companies or 'accounts'. Their brief is to help their corporate partners meet their objectives for charitable support by developing and managing tailor-made programmes. This approach can help build long-term relationships.

Seeking out new business opportunities and making initial approaches to companies may be the responsibility of each corporate fundraiser, or that of the head of corporate fundraising. Some charities, however, have re-organised to take account of the different set of skills that are needed for new business work. Macmillan Cancer Relief, for example, has corporate development managers, who seek out new business, and corporate fundraising managers, who account-manage projects.

Another trend is that of charities, such as Macmillan Cancer Relief, seconding corporate fundraisers to the companies they are in partnership with, to manage specific larger projects.

## How corporate fundraising links with and affects other areas of fundraising

For a strategy of corporate fundraising to work, everyone from the trustees down has to be committed to the programme and to investing the time and resources needed to make a success of it.

---

[1] 'Gifts in kind 1999/00': www.dsc.org.uk/corporatecitizen/spr00/topchart.htm#table1

Far from being an isolated team within a charity, the corporate fundraising department should work closely with other fundraising departments and be fully supported by the charity's functional departments.

The impact on all areas of operation for a charity undertaking a corporate fundraising programme can be considerable:

- The service provision side of the charity will need to communicate projects suitable for corporate support and be prepared to host visits for, or give presentations to, existing and potential corporate donors.

- The accounts department needs to be geared up to receive corporate donations and be fully conversant with the relevant tax laws.

- The company secretary may need to advise on the legal aspects of corporate fundraising; if the charity is going to be involved in sponsorship or promotions, the company secretary should advise on whether a trading company should be set up, to avoid corporation tax.

- The PR department should work closely with the corporate fundraisers to generate PR for partnerships and to ensure that the publications and messages being communicated are appropriate for the corporate market place.

- A charity-wide database is essential to cross-reference donors and track all interrelationships; this will require the input and support of the charity's IT expertise.

- All fundraising departments should liaise closely to ensure that donors have one key worker and are not bombarded with mass approaches from different fundraisers. Communication with contacts should be entered into a networked database. In particular, the relationship between the national and regional corporate fundraising operations has caused headaches for some charities and needs careful consideration.

# Ways to improve your corporate fundraising

A charity seeking to raise money from the corporate sector needs to be able to demonstrate why a company should support its cause rather than another. A clear understanding of a charity's unique selling propositions (USPs) is therefore vital, as is an investment in promotional materials such as a corporate brochure and a credentials document for presentations to potential supporters.

## Investing in research

Research is a vital means for the corporate fundraiser to keep informed of developments and key personalities in the corporate world, and of voluntary-sector news. For this reason, some of the larger charities have a researcher based in the corporate fundraising department.

Research is employed by some of the larger charities as a valuable way of gaining a clear picture of a charity's supporters, its level of awareness and its reputation with the public – and it need not be costly: for example, adding questions about a charity to an omnibus survey is an inexpensive exercise.

## Using PR

Companies are more likely to support a well-known charity that has the potential to generate interest and publicity for joint initiatives, particularly in the case of CRM. Becoming better known in the business world can therefore give a charity the edge.

A charity can increase its profile by submitting press releases to targeted media about existing partnerships and successes, organising events (for example, receptions) specifically aimed at the corporate world, and using influential supporters to spread the word.

A more expensive option is to invest in advertising directly for potential corporate partners, a route that has been pursued by a number of charities, such as the RSPCA. Advertising over a sustained period can be effective in generating awareness of the charity and keep a charity in the front of the minds of corporates seeking a partnership.

Many corporate partners will have a particular need for publicity, and it is therefore important that the corporate fundraiser can draw on the resources of the charity's communications specialists. Some charities have fulfilled this need by allocating a PR officer to major projects, or even having a dedicated corporate fundraising PR professional. Charities without this resource should make it clear that the company will need to use its own publicity machine.

## Networking and business groups

For every successful partnership a fundraiser builds, he or she is likely to have to make many unsuccessful approaches. Developing opportunities to open up a dialogue with potential partners is a vital way of increasing the likelihood of success. As competition gets more and more fierce, the personal approach is the one that stands the greatest chance of success.

A number of charities have set up a 'development board' or 'industry committee' of 'the great and the good' to help them make friends and influence people in the corporate sector and to open doors to companies. Any charity, whatever its size, can use its contacts and pulling power to involve senior industry personnel, and can take full advantage of the concept of a development board.

A board can operate on a formal basis, with regular collective meetings, or it may be a committee in name only: in this case, the fundraiser meets members individually and uses their expertise and contacts on an ad-hoc basis. Whichever approach is taken, the important thing is that the members of the board are committed to the charity and agree to help with contacts, advice and, possibly, ideas. In some cases, the board may also be actively involved in fundraising or in hosting events. The Lymphoma Association's Business Advisory Group, for example, helped host an exclusive private art viewing. As a result of a contact brought along by a member of the group, the charity ultimately won a £250,000 corporate partnership.

The success of a board depends on recruiting a good, and influential, chair. A good chair will have plenty of his or her own contacts to bring to the charity, and will motivate and lead members, helping the board achieve its potential. The NSPCC's FULL STOP Campaign provides an excellent example of an appeal that has made extensive use of high-level supporters and networking techniques: its winning combination has the Duke of York as overall chair of the campaign, supported by boards representing different industry sectors.

It must be stressed, however, that, although a charity's development board can be used to open doors, once the fundraiser has his or her foot in the door, the figures must stack up. Any proposed project is likely to be scrutinised by the relevant department within the company and must stand on its own merits.

## Who should sit on the board?

The seniority of those invited on the board will vary according to the charity's needs and the accessibility of the contacts available to it, but members should clearly be decision makers and budget holders within their companies. It is important to target people of a common level of seniority so they feel they are being asked to join a peer group.

Most people are flattered to be asked to join a board, especially where the chair is someone they admire, and may welcome the opportunity to network informally with other business people. However, some 'names' are in great demand from charities: investing in research to identify up-and-coming entrepreneurs can pay dividends. Equally, keeping an eye open for personal information about the rich and famous in the media can be fruitful: the most committed members tend to be people who have a personal interest in the work of the charity.

A development board needs regular maintenance to work to peak efficiency, since the charity is likely to be secondary to the main priorities of the board members. Specify what members are required to do and spoon-feed them where necessary: for example, when asking members for contacts, a draft list on which they can indicate who they know can be very helpful.

Each charity must determine the exact role of its board and its potential. Management of the board will be time consuming and, if not properly directed or chaired, the board may be little more than a pleasant talking shop. To ensure that the board meets its potential it must have clear objectives and be regularly evaluated.

Other networks available for a charity to exploit for corporate fundraising include the contacts of its trustees, its existing supporters and its suppliers.

## Major donors

According to the Pareto Principle, in any marketing exercise 80 per cent of business comes from 20 per cent of a company's customers: this is also true of corporate fundraising.

Identifying a charity's key or 'major donors' enables it to concentrate on the areas where there is the greatest chance of long-term income. This applies to individual major donors as it does to corporate major donors. It is the reason why the corporate fundraiser must know if the director of a target company is an individual donor in his or her own right, so that the approach may be tailored accordingly and the individual not bombarded with appeals from different areas of the charity.

Where fundraisers managing corporate donors and those managing major donors work closely together to identify opportunities, there is greater potential to maximise fundraising and contacts. Individuals can play key roles across the fundraising divide: for example, the chairman of an industry committee who is the managing director of a corporate supporter can also be developed as a major donor.

# Measuring success

## Evaluating corporate projects

A charity that monitors and evaluates each project it is involved in will be in a strong position to build on its successes and to use this information to increase support from existing and potential supporters. For example, producing a review document of a sponsorship activity detailing how objectives were met and what benefits were received by the company and the charity can help the former make a positive decision about future involvement. Presentation of this document will also give the charity an opportunity to schedule a meeting with the company.

## Evaluating corporate fundraising strategy

Some charities use benchmarking to evaluate their fundraising strategy, including that of the corporate fundraising operation. 'Fundratios' are a benchmarking tool, developed by the Centre for Interfirm Comparison, that allows evaluation of a charity's performance against that of other charities in a number of areas, for example in terms of how much each fundraiser raises. However, such statistics come with a health warning: charities have different ways of calculating expenditure and income, so like is not always compared with like.

What is vital is that the means for monitoring and evaluating a project form part of the plan drawn up by the corporate fundraising department (which will also outline objectives and strategy) and that each team member takes responsibility for their part in achieving this plan.

## Evaluation of CCI by companies

More and more companies are evaluating their support of charities against set objectives. Charities operating in the area of corporate fundraising must have an understanding of the various methods of evaluation used by companies and must ensure that they are working with companies to achieve the desired outcomes. (For more on this, see Chapter 4.)

## Assessing profitability

Success in corporate fundraising does not happen overnight, and a charity may have to make a considerable investment for it to work. The charity's trustees must therefore understand and support the long-term nature of corporate fundraising (in turn determined by company budget lead times) and the need to invest resources and have professionally trained staff. It is unrealistic to expect an investment in corporate fundraising to start paying off before year 3.

After such an initial set-up period, many charities use an income/cost ratio to evaluate their fundraising activities: NSPCC, for example, uses a ratio of 4:1 on its normal ongoing fundraising (this would not include special Appeal Fundraising, such as the FULL STOP Campaign, which would be expected to achieve a much higher return on investment).

It must be appreciated that any new initiative, for example embarking on a corporate mailing programme, is unlikely to achieve a ratio as high as 4:1 in the early stages. This is not to say that such initiatives are not worth the investment – they are often valuable ways of developing new areas of activity or of innovation – merely that such investment should not be made on the assumption of an immediately high income/cost ratio. Indeed, a recent survey shows many of the bigger charities spending well over 25p in the pound on corporate fundraising.[2]

# Conclusion

A properly managed, well-resourced corporate fundraising department – with good account management, a successful new business strategy, and an eye for new opportunities – has the potential to bring rich rewards to a charity. Efforts spent on developing major corporate donors and building long-term relationships with companies are likely to be a good investment since, with increasing competition, the most successful charities are those that look after their corporate partners best.

---

[2] 'Expenditure on corporate fundraising 1999/00': www.dsc.org.uk/corporatecitizen/spr00/topchar.htm#table10

# CHAPTER FOUR

# Evaluation

**Liz Markus**

# The central significance of evaluation

*Good intentions are not enough. Customers, investors, employees and stakeholders want demonstrable proof of action and improvement.* (Business Impact Report 2001, HRH Prince of Wales)

Active evaluation is key to any successful corporate fundraising operation. It will help you target your efforts and budgets more effectively and it will place you in a better position to maintain high-value relationships with your corporate partners. As a manager of corporate fundraising, tracking and evaluation will be a central part of ensuring your work is effective both for your corporate partners and ultimately for your cause. Keeping abreast of corporate discussions on evaluation may also prove useful in bringing new models of best practice to your own cause.

Evaluation does not need to be complex. It may help to see it as responding to two very simple questions: 'Did we succeed in doing what we set out to achieve?' and 'What can we learn for the future?'

In this chapter, we will be focusing on the evaluation of specific corporate fundraising partnerships. There are four sections:

- An overview of where evaluation currently fits into the corporate community affairs agenda
- An introduction to one of the main models that companies are now adopting in the UK (and signposts to other models)
- A framework for evaluation reports
- A summary of six key elements for success.

# Pressures on community affairs managers to evaluate

In a survey of the 'Most Respected Companies' carried out by Financial Times/PricewaterhouseCoopers, 750 chief executives across Europe were asked to comment on the most important business challenges for companies in the year 2000. Of those challenges listed, **increasing pressure for social responsibility** was ranked second only to the recruitment of skilled staff.

Government, consumers, investors and potential recruits are all looking for hard evidence on which to assess a company's commitment to society and the environment. Research shows that these assessments directly influence behaviour towards the company and have a direct impact on the financial bottom line. Community affairs is entering the mainstream of business, and companies are looking to make it more professional and more accountable. In 2001 it is anticipated that 70 per cent of FTSE 100 companies will be publishing reports on their corporate social responsibility (CSR). In order to do this, they need hard facts and evidence of success from their partners – and corporate fundraisers are one of the crucial links in providing them with this information.

*Measurement is not a hot topic; it is a way of life, particularly in business. Companies are performance-driven organisations, and if Corporate Community Investment specialists want to be part of the business mainstream they must talk the worldwide language of business, the language of output numbers.* (David Logan, Corporate Citizenship Company)

This is a new culture, for corporate partners as well as for fundraisers. If you can understand the environment in which your partners are operating, and anticipate their need for evaluation and feedback, you will be offering them a service which, in itself, will set you apart from others as a preferred partner. There are many corporate community affairs managers who will be providing social reports for the first time and may suddenly find that they lack the hard data they need to prove they are having a real impact. They will be heavily reliant on those charity partners who have provided them with full evaluation reports without their ever having asked for them.

# Leading the way in evaluation – the London Benchmarking Group model

One of the key influences in the area of evaluation has been a group of companies called the London Benchmarking Group. The group initially consisted of six companies who wanted to find new ways of measuring and assessing the effectiveness of the investments they were making in the community. The group has since grown to 52 companies (2001), and the model it developed for measuring corporate community involvement (CCI) looks set to become the standard among most leading companies.

The model describes four different categories of investment, each anticipating a different kind of return for the company (see Figure 4 for a summary of these categories). The group has developed a template for monitoring and measuring community involvement activities.

**FIGURE 4** THE LONDON BENCHMARKING GROUP MODEL

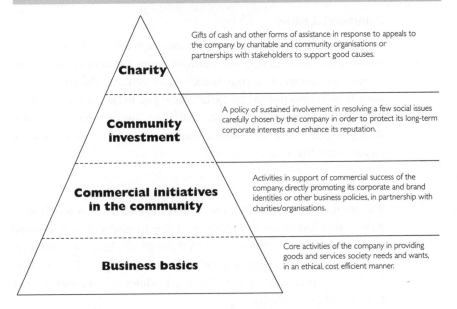

**Charity**
Gifts of cash and other forms of assistance in response to appeals to the company by charitable and community organisations or partnerships with stakeholders to support good causes.

**Community investment**
A policy of sustained involvement in resolving a few social issues carefully chosen by the company in order to protect its long-term corporate interests and enhance its reputation.

**Commercial initiatives in the community**
Activities in support of commercial success of the company, directly promoting its corporate and brand identities or other business policies, in partnership with charities/organisations.

**Business basics**
Core activities of the company in providing goods and services society needs and wants, in an ethical, cost efficient manner.

The London Benchmarking Group has drawn up a system of evaluating both inputs and outputs in these areas,[1] the main implications of which for your work as a corporate fundraiser are given here.

---

[1] These systems are not described in detail in this chapter; for further information, go to the group's own reports or visit its website:
www.corporate-citizenship.co.uk/benchmark

### Cash value

In calculating **inputs**, the company is looking to assess the value of all its contributions – not just cash, but also gifts in kind, staff time and expertise and other resources donated. You can help the company by assessing the total value of the donations to your cause.

It is in the area of measuring **outputs** that the company will rely heavily on feedback from its community partners. The company is looking to quantify outputs in terms of leverage, commercial gains and social impact.

### Leverage

By investing £10,000 in your cause, how much has the company helped you to 'lever in' from other sources? Has any matched statutory funding followed? Has its donation helped generate other gifts from corporate donors? The more you can show that the money will have a multiplier effect, the more motivating your feedback to the company will be.

### Commercial gains

Has the company gained anything commercially in return for its investment? Have its staff, for example, gained new skills as a result of their involvement in your work? Have you introduced the company to new commercial contacts? Have you helped it communicate its key messages to a new target audience? Any commercial returns that you can prove will help a company justify its investment in terms of the financial bottom line.

### Social impact

It is often easy to forget that companies need to see how much of an impact their donation has made, in order to justify their continued investment in the community. Even if the involvement is a commercial deal, they are partnering with a cause, and they will be looking for both factual and emotive feedback about the difference they have made to your work.

Companies are looking for different kinds of return for each of the four different types of investment:

- If the gift is a charitable one, the measurement should focus on the benefit to the community, not the company.
- If the involvement is community investment, the company will be interested in measuring benefits to both community and corporate partners.

- In cause-related marketing campaigns, the company will be focusing on the business benefits in any evaluation of success, rather than the benefits to the charity.

You will need to adapt your evaluation model to fit whichever of these the company is aiming for.

Corporate discussions within the London Benchmarking Group are now moving forward to tackle the challenge of measuring long-term **outcomes**, rather than simply quantifying short-term outputs: for example, in a project that may have ensured that 5,000 children are given support in their reading, what has the real impact been on reading levels and employment prospects for those children when they leave school? And, in the longer term, what is the impact on the community as a whole? Outcomes are much harder to assess, because they demand a longer time frame, but they are, nonetheless, of more importance than the initial outputs.

## Other corporate models

There are a number of other models currently influencing corporate thinking; the following web sites offer further details. This is a changing environment, and you will find it time consuming to follow every new angle of the debate; but if you choose one or two of these sites as regular favourites you should find that you are able to keep up with the key trends.

### www.bsr.org

Business for Social Responsibility, a US-based corporate membership organisation, has produced a guide to nine currently used external codes in 'A comparison of selected corporate social responsibility related standards'. The site also offers a useful summary of latest trends in community involvement.

### www.business-impact.org

Many leading influences in the area of corporate community activity are involved in the Business Impact Taskforce, chaired by BT's managing director: Business in the Community, the Department of Trade and Industry, Tomorrow's Company, Ashridge and many others. The Taskforce's full report, published in November 2000, is available on this site, which also offers free access to a resource bank of support materials and news.

## www.efqm.org

The European Foundation for Quality Management is highly influential in mainstream business, with over 90 per cent of the top *Times* 500 companies using some form of Total Quality Management. In order to win the prestigious international award, companies need to score at least 40 per cent in each of nine categories, one of which is focused on their 'Impact on Society' results.

## www.bnw.co.uk

Formerly Bruce Naughton Wade, this consultancy firm is now known as Probus BNW. The firm's Corporate Community Involvement Index preceded the London Benchmarking Group initiative, and focuses on benchmarking the processes, as well as the results, of community affairs programmes.

## www.Accountability.org.uk

The Institute of Social and Ethical AccountAbility launched the AA1000 framework in November 1999 and updates it regularly. AA1000 aims to provide a standard form for all social audits to ensure they are comparable and transparent.

## www.corporate-citizenship.co.uk

The Corporate Citizenship Company authored the London Benchmarking Group reports. They produce *Community Affairs Briefing*, which is the most widely read news journal for Community Affairs Managers.

## www.unitedutilities.com

This is a useful example of stakeholder-led evaluation with easy-to-download Impact on Society reports. United Utilities focus their evaluation according to their five Ps: Performance, Partnership, Processes, Participation and Perception.

## www.co-operativebank.co.uk

Award-winning Partnership Reports, available from this site, give a very clear view of current best practice in social reporting.

# A framework for an evaluation report for a corporate partner

There is no right or wrong format for a report, so do not feel bound by a rigid structure; adapt it to highlight the areas of strength in your own project. Below is a very brief outline, intended to help prompt your own thoughts.

Ideally an evaluation report should be presented face to face, and the written report handed over in the course of the meeting for the company to keep on record and to circulate internally. Presenting your evaluation in a meeting will allow you to discuss what has been learnt, how the company perceives the results and what might be possible in the future.

## Background

Always include a brief summary of the relationship, the longevity of past support and a reference to any other current forms of support you are receiving from across the company. Assume no prior knowledge; this will ensure that your contact will be able to circulate the report without having to provide their own briefing notes or introduction. It also means that, if staff changes occur, as so often happens, there are clear notes on record.

## Objectives

Summarise each of the objectives that your corporate contact cited at the beginning of your discussions. Include your own charity's objective(s) for the specific activity. Rather than presenting them separately as 'charity objectives' and 'company objectives', try to show that they have become shared and that both parties were aiming to deliver on each other's objectives as part of the partnership.

## Summary of activities

A brief, bullet-point summary of the activities that have taken place over the current period of evaluation will serve as a briefing, and can also provide a good reminder to the company of the energy and resources that you have invested in the project.

## Results for Community Partner X

Outline the results for the community partner first. Try to be as broad as possible in your assessment of the value. The more you can make the company feel it has generated benefits for you, the more it will see their investment as good value, and the more they will feel motivated to continue in the future.

Your results might include:

- funds raised or money saved;
- leverage (money raised/saved from others as result);
- leads (any future support that may be generated as result);
- qualitative feedback from participants/customers/beneficiaries (e.g. quotes showing positive attitudes towards the cause);
- social impact (what difference will it make to the work of the charity?) – try to make this specific and emotive, even if the relationship is a commercial one.

### Results for Company Y

Did you help the company achieve its objectives? Do you have evidence to prove that your partnership delivered any of the following?

- Raised the company's profile
- Boosted morale
- Team-built
- Developed staff skills
- Increased sales
- Reduced costs
- Increased traffic (e.g. number of customers in-store/visitors to website)
- Built 'brand equity' by association
- Created platforms for dialogue with national or local opinion formers
- Improved supplier relations
- Enhanced the company's image/reputation
- Generated positive media coverage
- Retained the company's 'licence to operate'

If the company has evaluated its own programme, do not give it feedback on what it already knows. More frequently, however, you will find that the company has not tracked its own investment, and is not aware of the real success of your partnership. In such circumstances, you need to provide as much of this information as possible – a difficult task, since you will not always have the information available. This is where you need to use some creativity to ensure that you can provide as much as possible to go on record. (See page 44 for some ideas on how to measure success.)

### The future

If you manage to secure a meeting to deliver your evaluation report, you may not wish to include any written reference to future potential. It would be best to discuss options first and follow up the meeting with any written version.

However, if the report is the only communication you will have with the company, it may be worth adding a page formally expressing your hope that the relationship will continue.

### Sign-off

I think it is always worth ending with an emotive sign-off, a quote, or a photograph, which leaves the reader motivated about the cause.

Don't forget to add the basics – the date, the charity and your contact details at the end. Even if they are in the attached letter, they may get separated, and you want this document to act as a stand-alone reference for others within the company.

## Six key elements for success

### Be proactive in offering evaluation feedback to partners

For some corporate fundraisers, the first time they turn to the challenge of evaluation is when a company explicitly asks for an evaluation report. The best corporate fundraisers pre-empt this, and ensure that they are leading their corporate partners to consider evaluation, even if the corporate contact does not raise the subject. You are operating in an extremely competitive environment and, if you do not make the value of your project explicit in written format, you will inevitably lose out to others who do.

### Clarify what success means right at the beginning

Rationally, everyone agrees that one needs to be crystal clear about objectives right at the start of each project. In reality, it is a rare project in which both corporate partner and charity have clarified what they are really looking for.

This may be the first time that the corporate partner has worked with a charity, and it may initially feel reluctant to discuss its commercial objectives. Assuring it that you are happy for benefits to be two-way and asking straight questions about its potential aims will help prompt more information about its real objectives. It is important to clarify the position early, so that you can be honest about whether you think you can deliver.

## Agree how you will measure that success

Once you are clear about what you are aiming to achieve, you need to discuss *how* you will measure progress to provide evidence that success is achieved. For example, if one of the company's objectives is to raise consumer awareness of its new product range, will it be carrying out research? If not, how can you prove you did a good job? It is often at this point that both parties realise that the objectives are not measurable and they are forced to revise them. It is far better to do this at the start than find yourself faced with an impossible evaluation later on.

Which party will take responsibility for this tracking and evaluation, and who will fund it? It is still rare that a company is willing to invest much money in tracking success, which makes it difficult for charity partners to show they are delivering against goals. However, there are some lower-cost forms of tracking that charity partners can carry out themselves.

If the partnership is a promotional one, more often than not you will find yourself forced to rely on media coverage. This coverage is frequently a key factor in success in the eyes of the company, because editorial is not something that a company can purchase for itself. It is possible for your charity to employ a volunteer to trawl through the papers at the beginning of each day and photocopy or cut out any coverage. If you are a medium-sized to large charity, you may have a press office that already tracks the press coverage and will select the relevant cuttings for you over the promotional period.

Media coverage can be monitored in terms of:

- column inches
- number of articles
- headline mentions
- page position
- photographs
- audience reach (e.g. regional spread, profile of readership)
- key messages communicated

- favourability towards the company (positive, negative or neutral)
- timing of coverage – whether or not it coincided with your promotional activities.

Most companies will be happy to have a summary of which papers/TV/radio covered the promotion, followed by a copy of the press cuttings.

Audience research is another key measure used by companies in promotional activities. This research may be quantitative (e.g. adding a question onto an omnibus research questionnaire, or a wider corporate research project) or qualitative (with focus groups giving a more in-depth insight into motivations and perceptions). It is rare that a charity can provide worthwhile data, unless your organisation is large enough to be investing in wider research projects that can afford to include an extra angle.

An activity based around employee volunteering is easier to assess from within the charity. If, for example, you are hosting employee challenges (where staff teams are invited to complete volunteering activities in your charity over a short period), you should provide questionnaires to all staff at the end of the day. Keep these brief – they should be no more than one or two sides of A4. Questions should probe whether the employees feel they have learnt more than from previous commercial team-building exercises, whether they felt the day was worthwhile, what they have learnt, and what they would suggest for future challenges. Such quotes will provide valuable feedback for the company at no cost to you, and will inform you about how you may be able to adapt your own programme in the future. The quotes will also be useful in promoting the value of these activities to potential corporate partners in the future.

### Build relationships to ensure all parties are ready to deliver

One of the great benefits of corporate fundraising within the voluntary sector is that it can often act as a catalyst to encourage charities to become more professional and accountable. As the corporate fundraiser, you may find yourself having to bridge the divide between your charity's culture and that of your corporate partner. Your partner may expect to see facts and figures that the charity will find hard to deliver. It will fall to you to find honest and inspiring answers to those questions.

Corporate fundraisers who work as a detached team within a charity will find it almost impossible to rely on the rest of the charity to deliver against promises. You need to put effort and time into building relationships and understanding within your own charity, in order to guarantee that you can rely on their supporting you and providing the information and results you need for reporting back. Inductions, internal training and informal meetings are all useful in engendering a culture of communicating across divisional boundaries.

When you are working on a Charity of the Year relationship or cause-related marketing promotion with a regional network of company staff, you may rely on obtaining information about progress from a whole range of regional reps, both within your charity and within the company. One effective way to gain information from regional corporate staff on a regular basis is to introduce some kind of incentive scheme. Offering competitions, for example, league tables, certificates or prizes linked to a regular newsletter, will ensure that you are kept up to date with totals raised, or milestones achieved.

### Keep feedback simple

Your contacts within companies do not have time to digest large reports. They need the facts, clearly, and in a format that they can pass on directly to others in the business. They will breathe a sigh of relief if your report is succinct and easy to understand.

### Hard facts and feel-good

Your corporate partner will be looking for all available hard evidence. That is what it will need when called to account by internal or external stakeholders.

Do not forget the feel-good factor. You are not a marketing agency; you are working for a cause, and you need to leave the corporate partner with a motivating emotional picture of how valuable its support of your charity's work has been.

# CHAPTER FIVE

# Making corporate fundraising work – 'achieving the win–win scenario'

**Hilary Jacklin**

## Introduction

In its discussion of how to make corporate fundraising work, this chapter will look at:

- how to make the process of securing corporate funding a success;
- how to make the relationship with the funder work once the funding has been secured.

Successful corporate fundraising is often judged solely from the point of view of winning funds. Little acknowledgement is paid to the fact that it is only when both sides are happy at the end of the relationship that it can be deemed to have been successful.

The key to the whole process is finding a good fit between the voluntary organisation and the corporate partner. If at the outset both sides are happy with the basis on which the arrangement has been made and with exactly what each will be putting in and getting out of their involvement, then you have the makings of a successful partnership. Companies are becoming increasingly frank and sophisticated about their motivations for charitable support. They may, for example, choose to work with your organisation because the profile of their customers is similar to that of your donors, or because your organisation can give them some good PR opportunities. These motivations need to have been identified, and you should be confident that the arrangement will satisfy them. Alongside this you need to be happy that the rewards that your organisation will be reaping are satisfactory for the investment being made.

# The process

## Where do you start?

There are over 3.7 million companies, of which over 7,000 have in excess of 250 employees. So where do you begin? You need to draw up a target or hit list. There are many ways to do this, but you must choose a technique that suits your organisation.

Methods of building a list include:

- geographical location – you may want to select companies of all sizes which are local to the service that you run;

- affinity companies – those companies that offer a similar product to your own or have a link to what you do;

- size of company – you may decide to go for companies with large charitable budgets where the returns may be high;

- past supporters – for those organisations with some experience of corporate fundraising, you can look back at records of where your support has come from in the past, even if it was just a small donation or, for example, the purchase of Christmas cards;

- a matrix approach – this approach involves using several factors to find those companies with the most likelihood of supporting you.

Be realistic in your expectations of the number of companies you will be able to approach over a certain period of time. Think about putting together a calendar of approaches with numbers per month, building in time for research and for other opportunistic or reactive approaches (see below). In order to build your target list, you will need basic information on the company; the more detailed research comes later.

## Planning your approach

As earlier chapters have indicated, corporate fundraising methods are very varied, from straight philanthropic donations to complex promotions where the benefits to both sides can be significant. The company should be viewed as a multi-faceted resource with any number of routes through which you can make an approach. The varied nature of the potential funding will inevitably call for the use of differing methods to secure the income: for example, a request for a donation to pay for a piece of specialist equipment will be a lot more straightforward than putting together a complex pitch for a major charity of the year.

The key to all approaches is the 'fit', getting the combination of the right product/project with the right fundraising mechanism, which offers the company and your organisation the opportunity to meet their combined needs.

# Your charity's USPs

In building up your approach you will need to think about your charity's unique selling propositions (USPs). What can you offer that is different from others? This could be, for example, a particular project or service that is an attractive fundraising opportunity, a donor base that is significantly large, an interesting fundraising idea, or the strong links that you have with the media. Develop a list of your key selling points to draw from for each approach.

### The approach

With your target list in place and your ideas for propositions for funding thought through, it is now time to research the companies thoroughly – it is often quoted that a successful application is 60 per cent research and 40 per cent application. There is no substitute for comprehensive research.

### Research

For every company on your 'hit list', you need to have gathered the following kind of information:

- its business – is it in any way complementary to your own?
- its location (including any subsidiaries) – are its sites near your own?
- key personnel (including non-executive directors) – are any of them known to you or anyone associated with your organisation, such as your trustees or suppliers?
- its size, in terms of both turnover and numbers of employees – could it be a target for a charity of the year or employee fundraising initiative?
- its charitable policy and previous charitable involvement – does it have a structured charitable application process and formalised programme of charitable involvement? Which causes and types of charity is it interested in?
- its motivations for charitable giving – particularly where there is the potential for a large donation, pure philanthropy is rare;

- its current strategy – is it planning a major expansion or planning to downsize?

- ethics – does your organisation have any particular ethical policy (e.g. no association with alcohol or cigarette companies – see Chapter 8 for more information) that would make it inappropriate to be associated with that company?

This kind of information will help you to get a feeling for the suitability of an approach and how to frame it.

There are many sources available to research companies, for example published directories such as Dun and Bradstreet's *Key British Enterprises*, Hemmington Scott's *The Corporate Register* or the Directory of Social Change's *Guide to UK Company Giving*. These are updated every two years and should be available in larger libraries. The internet offers a wealth of information, from media reports on your target company to the company's own web site. There are also specific online systems such as Lexis Nexis (www.lexisnexis.com), which again should be available from libraries if you do not want to purchase them. Don't forget that a telephone call is an excellent way to gather and confirm information, and is also useful as a preliminary to building a rapport with the decision makers. Most of the FTSE 100 companies will have a department or an individual responsible for corporate community affairs, whose job it is to provide you with information and direction on making an approach. Where there is no such resource, speak to the receptionist, who should be able to send you an annual report or, for example, confirm job titles and names of key personnel.

Where possible, set up a short information-gathering meeting with those responsible for charitable giving/corporate/community affairs before making any written application.

# Types of proposal

## Written

There are two main types of written proposal: the bespoke or tailored proposal and the standard, mail-shot proposal. Both have their role, but each needs to be used appropriately. In both cases, you should try to avoid using jargon and acronyms, and including too much information.

### Bespoke or tailored proposals

Tailored proposals require considerable preparatory research to ensure that you are making a relevant approach; without this, you will be wasting your time and theirs. Communication with the company should direct you to what you should include in the proposal, but it is likely that you will need to cover some or all of the following:

- a brief synopsis of your organisation's purpose;
- a summary of the project to be funded;
- what the company will get out of the involvement – be specific, indicating, for example, the number of your donors that they will reach;
- the fundraising mechanism – how do you propose to raise the funds?
- what your organisation is offering – awareness, brand building, team building?
- what you are expecting from the company, and how it can get involved;
- budget, in terms of the investment to be made and the predicted outcome;
- credentials/testimonials – your charity's previous experience;
- why the company should chose your charity rather than any other.

## Standard proposals

The mail-shot approach obviously enables you to reach considerable numbers of potential donors; however, the payback is likely to be substantially smaller than with the tailored approach. You will again need to have done your research in advance to ensure that the company will consider your approach and, more importantly, that you are not 'inoculating' the company from giving you a much larger gift. Why ask for a raffle prize when you might be considered for a four-figure sum? A standard proposal document may cover similar information to that listed above for the tailored proposal, but in a briefer form. It should be accompanied by a personalised letter giving a very short synopsis of the proposal document. If, however, you are either making a non-specific request or asking for a small amount, then a straightforward letter to the decision maker would suffice.

You will be lucky if you get a big response from a mail-shot to companies, but the technique is worth using as a mop-up when you do not want to spend too much time on making an approach.

## Opportunistic approaches

One less-structured, and often-overlooked, method of corporate fundraising is opportunism. This relies on thinking creatively and being on the lookout for potential avenues. For example, a major retail chain may be about to open a store in your area selling a product that has an affinity to your own. They will be looking to launch the store, to build awareness and attract custom. Why not approach them with a fundraising idea that meets their needs and generates income?

All staff should be encouraged to look out for ideas and to make suggestions.

## Joint approaches

In the past there have been few examples of charities coming together to work jointly with companies. This is, however, likely to become increasingly popular with companies if they can be shown to be supporting a wider audience and thereby generating more funds or gaining greater exposure for similar effort. It is worth considering both complementary and similar organisations to your own when framing an approach. If you do go down this route, you need to be very clear at the outset how the relationship will work between the two charities. You must have clear lines of communication and be in agreement as to who will take responsibility for which parts of the deal.

## Personal relationships

The use of personal contacts can be helpful in making corporate fundraising work: your trustees, volunteers or board members may have useful contacts in decision-making roles in the corporate sector. If you are planning an approach, this extra link may be of immense value.

Personal relationships between the fundraiser and the company are also important. Sometimes these can take years to establish, with company and charity taking time to get to know each other and waiting for the right fundraising idea or project to come up.

## Pitches and presentations

More often than not a large-scale deal will require a presentation to the key decision makers. This presentation may be made alongside other shortlisted organisations and will follow the written presentation selection process.

Preparation is the key to making successful presentations or pitches. Research is again crucial in establishing what your audience wants to hear and what you should be covering in your presentation. You should have a clear idea of who you will be presenting to: if, for example, the chair or chief executive of the company will be attending, it may be appropriate for someone of similar seniority in your organisation to be present. You may need to think about asking a beneficiary of the service you provide, or someone who provides that service, to accompany you to the presentation – their first-hand experience may enable them to talk more knowledgeably, or more persuasively, about the service.

You should know how long the company will expect you to speak and what sort of audio-visual equipment will be available. You may need to think creatively about the treatment of the presentation: how are you going to stand out from your competitors?

How you pitch your presentation should be guided by the type of deal and the nature of the company. There is a marked difference between being professional and being perceived as slick. Charities need to retain and communicate their *raison d'être* and their empathy with their own particular cause. It may be appropriate to use an audio-visual presentation for some audiences, but totally inappropriate for others. The presenter must also be prepared to move away from his or her 'script', perhaps where questions require this.

It is all too easy when pitching to promise more than you know you can deliver in order to win the deal. You need to be honest about what your organisation can offer, for example in terms of resources or numbers of people you can reach.

# Making the relationship work

### The contract

After you have secured the funding, it is always advisable to draw up some kind of clearly articulated statement of expectation, agreed by both sides, for whatever kind or level of involvement. This gives both sides a clear framework from which to work and can prevent, or certainly minimise, dissatisfaction.

A contract should cover such issues as clarification of the project and its outcomes, minimum guarantees, the use of branding and financial arrangements. It could take the form of a letter or simple statement; in the case of a major sponsorship, promotion or complex deal, it could be a longer, legally drafted document. A contract should be drawn up by a legally qualified professional, preferably with relevant experience. (The cost of using lawyers should be taken into account when the deal is being negotiated.) In some instances, the contract will need to carry legally drafted wording on promotional material; this should be agreed, and responsibility for its correct use assigned.

Remember that you are equal partners in setting up the deal: the charity has as much right as the company to dictate terms on the use, for example, of its logo.

The contract can also be used to evaluate the success of a corporate partnership, providing the benchmarks by which it can be judged.

## Managing the relationship

Once the funding has been secured, the work really starts. The nature of the relationship and the type of fundraising mechanism employed will dictate the level of input required by both parties, and the contract or letter of agreement should detail the work expected on both sides. It is the charity's responsibility to deliver.

A major Charity of the Year partnership, for example, will involve extensive work to maximise its success, and you may need to give guidance to the company and its employees on how to achieve the targets. A corporate donation towards the purchase of a piece of equipment, on the other hand, may only require regular written reports on its use and perhaps a visit by the funder.

For each involvement, it is wise to establish an 'account manager' to be responsible for the management of the relationship, or a team of people if the partnership is resource intensive. It is important to have the appropriate level of contact: the account manager may, for example, be the key contact for the board members/community affairs director, but the day-to-day running of the account may be undertaken by someone in a more junior role.

Where the relationship extends over a period of time, you should schedule regular update and planning meetings. At the outset there should be clear guidelines as to how the relationship will be evaluated, whether this is, for example, on the basis of income generated, awareness raised or skills developed.

It is important that charities act responsibly and professionally through the whole process of corporate fundraising. If expectations are not met, either as the result of unrealistic promises or lack of effort, this will cause frustration and bad feeling, which will reflect badly on your organisation and the sector as a whole.

# Conclusion

Corporate fundraising is one of the most interesting and creative of fundraising techniques. It can also be hugely lucrative and offers excellent cost ratios. However, to make a success of it, you need to remember that every voluntary organisation is unique, and so too is every company. While this offers plenty of scope for everyone to develop different mechanisms to raise funds, it also means that every relationship will require different handling. This chapter has tried to provide some pointers in how to be successful, but there can be no broad-brush formula to successful corporate fundraising – it requires time, effort and creativity, and a little luck.

# CHAPTER SIX

# Corporate fundraising mechanisms

**Rachel Billsberry-Grass and Manny Amadi**

## Employee fundraising – the benefits and drawbacks *Rachel Billsberry-Grass*

As its name suggests, employee fundraising is where the employees of a company team together to raise money for a charity. One particularly enthusiastic staff member could be the inspiration behind employee fundraising, or it could be more formalised, with a company choosing an adopted charity each year and encouraging its employees to support it.

## Benefits

The charity can gain a huge amount of money from employee fundraising (amounts of £100,000–£1 million are not uncommon), which is an excellent way to build strong and lasting links with a company, its customers and suppliers, all of whom are likely to be involved in one way or another. The direct access to employees means a charity can motivate and inspire, with potential long-term benefits.

It is also an opportunity to generate press coverage in the local, regional or even, on occasion, national press.

The company will also benefit from its association with the charity. Through general promotion of the partnership (posters, leaflets, web sites, logo on headed paper, etc.) and press coverage, the company will send a positive message to both existing and potential employees and customers.

The involvement of customers could even be used to encourage future footfall in the company's outlets, for example by running fundraising activities that require a repeat visit to a shop, such as a children's colouring competition.

The company could use employee fundraising as a development tool for its staff, whether for team building or as a secondment opportunity for an individual (to manage the partnership).

## Drawbacks

Inevitably, however, there are some drawbacks, perceived or otherwise, for both the charity and the company.

For the charity, employee fundraising is likely to be time consuming, and could require a lot of investment up front, which is risky. The planning and motivating will require skill, patience and persistence, and somebody will need to have specific responsibility for managing the relationship with a company. The charity might need to supply resources such as posters, leaflets and collecting boxes, which could run into many thousands of pounds of up-front investment.

Employee fundraising can be risky in a broader sense, to the charity's reputation. If the initiative fails, the charity might find itself out of pocket and with a company trying to distance itself. If the charity's promises are not fulfilled (or even if the company has unrealistic expectations, which the charity does not address at the beginning of the relationship), the unhappy company is unlikely to provide a glowing reference to the charity's would-be future partners.

The company might also consider up-front investment (of money or staff time) to be a drawback. As a result, some companies will only allow their employees to do fundraising in their own time.

# Finding a partner

As with any fundraising, it is important to start with a strategy. When deciding whether employee fundraising can work for a charity, it must look internally and address a few key questions:

- What is the case for support? What does the charity need money for? Is this the kind of thing that will inspire a group of people to raise money?

- Does the charity have the necessary resources to handle an employee-fundraising partnership – staff time, materials, financial?

- What is the charity's timescale for raising the money? Employee fundraising is not generally a quick-fix option, and the charity will need time to plan, motivate and encourage.

Finding a partner, the next stage of the strategy, requires research. The charity will need to identify which companies already do employee fundraising, and which companies it might be able to persuade to try it. The charity should consider the following sets of questions:

- Are they likely to support the cause? Is there a natural fit? (Many of the companies that have existing employee-fundraising schemes will have criteria for which charities they will support – if the charity does not fit the company's criteria, a lot of time will have been wasted.)

- Who decides which charities to consider, and how can the charity influence this decision? Is it a senior executive who could be courted by a lunch with the charity's celebrity patron? Is it a charity committee, the individuals of which the charity should be getting to know? Is the final decision made by staff vote? Although staff votes often favour the very popular larger charities, this is not inevitably the case – a charity's contacts could be used to encourage colleagues to vote its way.

- Does the charity have existing corporate supporters who would try some employee fundraising and, if so, to whom should it speak?

When approaching a company, the charity must follow the company's suggestions for what information they need: how the charity meets the company's criteria, how it proposes to manage the relationship, fundraising ideas and so on. It is also important to clarify who the information is for – management, staff or both.

Commitment from the senior executives in the company (not just the staff) is vital, unless there is an exceptionally motivated and strong individual who is taking the lead. If the employees see the most senior people cycling 100 miles, or giving up part of the team meeting to discuss fundraising ideas, they are more likely to support the charity. If a company is unwilling to offer this, there will undoubtedly be a negative impact on the fundraising potential.

## Planning the initiative

The charity and the company should nominate individuals as the main points of contact and then agree the targets and objectives. The charity's main objective is likely to be financial; the company may be reluctant to agree a financial target but, if the charity is investing resources in the relationship, it is important that the company is aware of its expectations. On the other hand, some companies may agree to match all the funds raised, or in some situations will underwrite a minimum donation. Whatever the case, if the respective views of each partner are hopelessly out of kilter, the charity should be considering whether it will be cost effective enough to continue.

The fundraising period will need to be planned in some detail. If the charity has prepared a proposal, this can form the basis of a plan, although the company may have its own ideas of what it wants to do based on what has worked well for it in the past. During this stage, the various responsibilities and deadlines should be agreed, and everybody should understand that the project's success will depend on each individual's meeting his or her responsibilities by the required time.

It is good practice for the charity to have this all agreed in writing, ideally in a contract or agreement. Some companies will find this too formal; as a fallback option the charity should send a copy of the minutes asking the company to correct anything that it disagrees with.

## Managing the initiative

The most important thing for the charity to do is everything it has promised. If the charity has promised dedicated PR support, it should make sure this is provided (the company *will* expect results). If it has promised a permanently staffed helpline for employees, it should not use voicemail! And, if for any reason it proves impossible to meet some of the promises, the charity must inform the company at the earliest opportunity.

It is also extremely important for the charity to develop good relationships with key people in the company, having regular meetings and telephone calls. This will make it much easier to discuss any problems.

Together the charity and the company should monitor the initiative's progress and ensure that it is on track to meet its target, remaining flexible and open to new fundraising ideas if things start to go awry.

## Handling problems

Diplomacy is needed when handling problems – and no one approach works in all situations: every relationship depends on the nature of the individuals involved.

The charity should acknowledge its own mistakes but, if it feels that the root of a problem lies with the company, it will have to address this. A meeting to review plans can be used as an opportunity to refer back to the original document detailing the responsibilities that were agreed. If deadlines have been missed, new deadlines should be set; if fundraising events are not going well, new ones should be introduced. The charity should follow up the meeting with minutes and regular phone calls to monitor progress.

If things still do not improve, the charity will need to be direct about the company's original commitment and the charity's own investment in the initiative. Unfortunately, unless there is a signed agreement or contract, the charity can do very little to make the company 'solve' the problem (whether that means undertaking its promises in terms of encouraging employees, or making its promised minimum donation). It is therefore in the charity's interest to remain on good terms with the company and to try to find an amicable solution.

If, after attempts of this kind to resolve the problem, there is still no noticeable improvement, the charity should withdraw from the partnership before losing any more money.

# Evaluation

Ideally the charity and the company will review and evaluate the initiative together, by comparing the results against the aims. Occasionally the results considerably exceed the aims; when this happens, make sure it is clearly noted.

Success should be communicated to all involved in the initiative and should be celebrated in whatever way the charity and company decide is appropriate, for example an awards ceremony to which the media are invited. The charity should get quotes and references from the company that can be used in future pitches to other companies.

It is just as important to hold the review if things have not gone as well as hoped, so that both parties can use the relationship as a learning experience. The charity should undertake this exercise itself, whether or not the company chooses to be involved, in order to ensure that it has a clear view of how to plan and implement future employee fundraising initiatives, and of what it should expect of potential partners.

# Cause-related marketing *Manny Amadi*
## Definitions and dimensions

Even in the very early days of capitalism, some leading business entrepreneurs and captains of industry recognised the link between healthy, enduring businesses and the society in which they operate. Rowntree and Cadbury in the UK, and Carnegie and Rockefeller in the USA infused their organisations with the sort of business purpose that transcended short-term bottom-line profits. They were no selfless altruists. They merely recognised and applied the principle of enlightened self-interest – or the concept of win–win. Their businesses, though much changed, have endured over time.

The logic of enlightened self-interest on which their relationship with society was based has also survived.

Today corporate social responsibility (CSR), corporate citizenship or sustainable business are broad terms, essentially promoting the view that businesses are sustained by society and can in turn benefit from attempts to sustain the society in which they operate. Many businesses now work hard to manage their impact on society – from promoting positive practices internal to their organisations, to relating positively with the community – using tools and functions such as advocacy, human resources, marketing resources and spend, etc. Cause-related marketing (CRM) represents one aspect of this dynamic relationship between business and society.

There are many definitions of CRM, but the Business in the Community (BitC) definition is the most widely accepted. BitC defines CRM as 'a commercial activity by which businesses and charities or causes form a partnership with each other to market an image, product or service for mutual benefit'.

CRM is funded mostly from the marketing and commercial budgets of companies. As the definition implies, it requires the demonstration of tangible – and, ideally, measurable – benefit for the parties involved.

It is difficult to determine the amount of money UK corporates spend on – or how much the community benefits financially from – CRM activities. No robust figures exist. BitC has projected that CRM spend equates to at least 0.4 per cent of total marketing spend in the UK. Assuming UK total marketing spend of over £25 billion for the year 2000, this indicates CRM activity in the region of £100 million.

There is scope for contesting the specific accuracy of these indicative valuations. What cannot be in doubt is that, over recent years,

CRM has become an additional, and increasingly established, new source of income to charities and good causes, as marketing and commercial budgets, previously closed to corporate fundraisers, have become legitimately opened up to them.

# Benefits and challenges

Whether in the form of product or brand promotions (as in the *Sun/Walker* 'Books for Schools'), sponsorships (Prince's Trust/Capital Radio Party in the Park series, or Cancer Research UK/Tesco Race for Life), Affinity Cards (Halifax Visa and four charities), CRM activities can yield extensive benefits for good causes and their commercial partners. Some of these benefits are listed below:

### For businesses

- Awareness (corporate, brand, product, etc.)
- Enhanced reputation (corporate, brand, product, etc.)
- Increased sales
- Attracting and retaining customers (loyalty)
- Differentiation
- Better-motivated employees
- Positive relationships with legislators and regulators
- Tangible benefits for communities

### For non-profit organisations

- Awareness
- Increased income – from a growing source
- Broadened fundraising portfolio
- Enhanced reputation
- Improved profile
- Enhanced brand
- New channels of communication (via product, people, place, etc.)
- Leveraged funding opportunities
- Differentiation
- New partnerships (with potential for long-term relationships and extension into other products).

CRM is the only marketing activity that can achieve all the above benefits for businesses *and* deliver tangible benefits for good causes. The examples in Chapter 11 from the NSPCC highlight how these benefits are achieved.

In order to secure benefits, successful CRM campaigns follow a set of principles and criteria that, although no guarantee of success, significantly enhance their chances of success. Best known of these are the BitC principles or rules of engagement set out in Annabel James's NSPCC examples later on in this book.

Despite its many virtues, CRM operates in the real world, and life, as we know, is not perfect. Even in circumstances where sound planning and preparation have been undertaken, things can, and do, go wrong. Sometimes this can be because external factors – economic downturn, take-overs or mergers, etc. – intrude. Sometimes things go wrong as a result of poor planning, lack of 'fit' between corporate and good-cause partners (a serious error), or for other reasons.

In addition to these, CRM has some inherent dynamics that potential players of the game – particularly good causes – should keep in mind. First, with some notable exceptions, such as Tesco Computers for Schools and Party in the Park, most campaigns – even highly successful ones such as the *Sun*/Walker 'Books for Schools' – tend to be short term in nature, so that the leverage that could be gained over a longer time period is often lost. This phenomenon is linked to the fact that corporate marketers, who are typically in their roles for two years, seek a quick 'trophy' before they move on.

This is linked to the danger that good causes should always watch out for, which is that they can be used cynically by companies, their brands and products as 'fig leaves' to divert attention from, or 'clean up', their organisation's transgressions or to enhance dubious reputations. The irony of a major cigarette manufacturer sponsoring a UK university's Centre for Corporate Social Responsibility and the collateral harm that is causing the university is well documented.

Second, although great and enduring relationships require a fair balance of power, the relationship between business and good-cause partners is often lop-sided in favour of commercial organisations. This is often a result of the sheer fact that those holding the purse strings are perceived to hold all the aces. This can be circumvented by good causes working hard to gain a market understanding of the value of their own brand, product, event, etc. (a number of the leading CRM charities are beginning to seek third-party guidance in valuing their portfolio of assets – this helps them to negotiate with confidence). It takes an enlightened and far-thinking corporate partner to realise that the charity's benefit can also bene-fit them, if they are interested in playing a long-term game.

A final key factor to bear in mind is that CRM is funded from mar-keting and commercial budgets. This means that, unlike, say, cor-porate donations, charities have a wider competitive set that includes promotions agencies, advertising and PR agencies, and others. Clearly, it requires a higher degree of professionalism and smart thinking on the part of good causes to beat these new com-petitors in a tough game. To their credit, many charities win, and do so on small budgets – sometimes with outside help and some-times without. If your charity has a commercial advisory group or sub-committee, use the members as sounding boards. If not, set up such a group, or find appropriate external support.

## Planning the campaign

Charity fundraising managers who want partners from the corpor-ate world must be prepared to go out and find those partners, and not expect businesses to come to them. Indeed, they must become as proficient at marketing their organisations as corporations are at marketing themselves. It is therefore vital for fundraising managers to have a well-developed strategy, to know exactly what the nature of the product they hope to sell is – its social, political, and economic advantages to the business world – and to have an approximate programme value in mind. This should be evaluated as any spon-sorship programme would be – through an analysis of reach, and of the campaign's marketing strength.

## The fit

Above all else, it is essential that charities court commercial part-ners that have a genuine link to the cause. A CRM campaign where there is not a clear link, or 'fit', is very unlikely to achieve its object-ives. Frank Bulgarella, a US CRM expert and veteran of the Special Olympics programmes, has no doubt that developing the right part-nership is the most important element of CRM: 'The link of the cause is what makes the sale.' In the USA, where surveys reveal that 93 per cent of firms declare that they engage in CRM, this development of the link has become a marketing art form. Ameri-can Express has developed a regular fourth-quarter annual cam-paign called 'Charge against Hunger' – the greatest strength of which is the company's consistency; Starbucks Coffee has produced $20 sampler bags with $2 of every sale going to the promotion of coffee growing in Ethiopia, Guatemala, Kenya and Indonesia.

**10 questions for a charity to ask before entering into a CRM relationship with a commercial partner**

- Is the idea you're promoting mutually beneficial? Does it fit into the ethos of both your organisations?

- Have you got the time and resources to manage the programme properly? Does it bring both partners desired rewards?

- Can you assure consumers that the partnership is sincere? Does it seem cohesive?

- CRM works on an emotional level. Will your campaign actively engage the consumer?

- Are the company's senior executives positive about the project?

- Is the company prepared to devote enough time and money to furthering the project?

- Have you established the proper parameters of the relationship? Do you know what to expect from each other? Who is to manage the delivery of the programme, media relations, finance, etc?

- Have you explored whether the company is willing to involve its employees as well as its suppliers, dealers, franchises, etc?

- Will you have the space to pursue your activities properly?

- Have you drawn up a legal, binding contract?

# Looking ahead

So, CRM is making a mark for business and good causes. Playing the CRM game has many challenges, some of them significant and culturally sensitive. There are, however, considerable benefits to be gained, as the examples which follow illustrate. Looking into the future, CRM seems set to endure and grow over time. It will do so because of its core essence, as highlighted by the Cadburys and Rowntrees of yesteryear. It is built on mutual benefit, or the concept of enlightened self-interest. This explains why it will continue to grow.

# CHAPTER SEVEN

# Structuring corporate fundraising

**Jeremy Hughes**

## Introduction

Most fundraising charities recognise funds from companies as a way of contributing to their annual voluntary income. As previous chapters have indicated, securing this income is more complex than simply asking for a donation: in order to earn as much income as possible over the long term, consideration has to be paid to the way in which corporate fundraising may best be structured. This chapter addresses this issue of structure, looking at it in terms of both human resources and systems. Because the corporate fundraising story is one of mistaken approaches as well as success, the examples in this chapter are attributed to no single charity.

One key point to be made here is that there are no uniform right answers to fundraising problems, and fundraising managers must constantly review their structure in the light of a changing climate of corporate giving and the evolution of their own charity's fundraising.

## Moving away from opportunism

Here is an approach to corporate donations with which corporate fundraisers may be familiar:

A major British company invited two corporate fundraisers to its London headquarters to make a 15-minute presentation to its chairman, company secretary and two other directors. They were to base their decision on which charity was to be the beneficiary of their annual £200,000 gift on the strength of those presentations.

This approach is to be condemned, not because one applicant is bound to be unsuccessful but because it suggests that, even if a corporate fundraiser approaches the presentation professionally, the result is primarily down to luck. Fortunately, cases such as this are increasingly rare; nevertheless, in many charities the belief may remain, among trustees in particular, that the secret to corporate fundraising success is opportunism and personal contact. The reality is that corporate giving is increasingly a result of design rather than accident: the gentleman's club does play a part, but the key is a professional fundraiser working within a structured programme and operation.

Fundraisers talk about managing finally to meet the chairpersons of large PLCs, only to be told that it is not they who decide which charity to support but the dedicated community affairs team, which operates within a clearly defined, and approved, strategy. This is the team with which the fundraisers have to develop a professional relationship if they are to succeed in securing a donation.

There are two main influences responsible for this state of affairs:

- increasing competition – more and more charities are entering the corporate fundraising market place, but corporate giving has not kept pace with the increasing demand;

- developing partnerships – a one-off donation may be solicited in an opportunistic fashion, but a partnership requires systems and structures if it is to be managed effectively.

# Establishing a corporate fundraising structure

The process of setting up an efficient corporate fundraising structure has four stages:

1 Assessing your charity's position vis-à-vis corporate fundraising and devising an appropriate strategy.

2 Agreeing a staffing structure to deliver the strategy.

3 Setting up systems for researching, gaining, managing and monitoring business.

4 Evaluating and, most importantly, reviewing your structure in the light of experience.

The first of these is covered in detail in Chapter 5 (see p. 47); the others are discussed below.

## Agreeing a staffing structure

A charity employing its first corporate fundraiser is likely to recruit a specialist to work in a central fundraising team. This person increasingly holds the key to successful corporate giving, but care is needed in selecting that fundraiser and attention given to whether further corporate fundraisers may be needed.

The formulation of an appropriate staffing structure hinges on answering the following questions:

- What is your target market for corporate fundraising (e.g. large or small companies? what is the geographical coverage?)?

- What corporate fundraising 'products' are appropriate for your charity (e.g. cause-related marketing, employee fundraising, donations, gifts in kind)?

- What methods will you be employing to generate new business (e.g. will it be coming from existing, 'warm' contacts or will it need to be generated 'cold'?)?

- How will your corporate fundraiser(s) 'fit' with other fundraisers (staff and volunteers)?

The answers to these questions will help to clarify the skills you will need in your corporate fundraiser or your corporate fundraising team. Thereafter, you need to decide how to distribute these skills. Should every member of staff be able to work with any company and any product? Or would it be more effective to have specialists with certain skills? If you have a corporate fundraising team, or are creating one, should the team be regionally based, centrally based, or a combination of the two – for example, with a central team handling 'product management' or new business?

Central structures can in general be implemented simply and can work effectively. The difficulty arises when you then attempt to lock this into a charity's regional or local operation. Historically, regional corporate fundraising was often undertaken by staff or volunteers seeking one-off funding for a particular piece of equipment or event. It was often assumed that the same resources could simply be tapped again each year. To take one example: a major summer fête was always supported by the local bank, which displayed banners with their logo. The bank had always 'supported' rather than 'sponsored', giving gifts in kind (e.g. printing) rather than cash. Nobody questioned, year on year, whether another sponsor might offer more, or whether the existing sponsor might be asked to give more.

There are also examples of corporate fundraising being added to the responsibilities of a community fundraiser. This system has the potential to work, but in practice it requires substantial investment and a recognition that the skills and experiences needed to be a good community fundraiser are often not the same as those required for a corporate fundraiser. In addition, it requires very clear lines of demarcation and communication. Some cases, such as adoption as Charity of the Year by a major retailer, may require the fixed-term appointment of a corporate fundraiser to lead the relationship. That 'account handler' will, however, only achieve the year's potential if they can call on the support and active involvement of fundraisers in all parts of the charity.

## Setting up systems

It is rare to find a charity that has kept adequate historical records of corporate giving. In one charity, tidy-minded administrative staff cleared out all the 'old paperwork' belonging to a capital appeal fundraiser when he left on achieving his £1.5 million target. Corporate fundraisers will be used to piecing a picture of previous activity together by trawling fundraising department records, finance department records, reports, minutes, press cuttings and the memories of long-standing staff and volunteers. These last often reveal the most – typically that what appears to be a personal gift is in fact a donation from a company, and vice versa. Commonly omitted from the records are major capital appeals conducted with the help of external fundraising consultants; and yet some of the largest corporate gifts are to be found in precisely this area. Record keeping relates not just to what was received, but to who was instrumental in securing the result. A charity, for example, had cases of company gifts resulting from: an indirect approach via an employee who had benefited from the charity's services; a partner in a leading legal firm twisting a client's arm; and an individual who first supported the charity through Rotary and then took their enthusiasm back into the company. In all these cases, personal contact provided a fertile ground, to which the professional fundraiser had to add the essential ingredients of a well-researched case for support and professional presentation.

This information must be translated onto a database system that, ideally, cross-refers individual involvement to corporate contacts and, ultimately, to corporate support. How to select an appropriate database is more than a chapter in its own right: suffice to say that it is both an issue of system software and also the training and practice of fundraisers in the use of that software. The level of investment may be considerable, especially if fundraisers who are based far away from head office are provided with online access to a central database.

# Issues of responsibility and demarcation

The demarcation issues mentioned above need to be addressed through a clearly defined policy on responsibilities and areas of operation. One fundraiser reports that a major national retailer refused to make a donation because four requests from different parts of the charity all ended up at head office. The retailer told the fundraiser that they did not see it as their job to sort out which part of the charity's work they should support. Another fundraiser discovered that no one was raising funds from businesses in the Doncaster area despite the fact that the city was within easy striking distance of three of the charity's projects: each fundraiser had assumed that another fundraiser covered that area. This is a clear demonstration of how a lack of appropriate systems can lead to lost opportunities.

The simplest way to address this issue is to have a database that identifies key workers for each company and which all fundraisers have to check in advance of any approach. The database can also be used to identify regularly which companies have not been approached, or for which no approach is planned. In practice, because of the difficulties of dealing with brands and subsidiary companies, larger charities with active local networks find that disputes often arise. In such a context, a 'traffic light' system has resolved the issues. A red-light company may only be approached by the designated head-office fundraiser, because there is evidence of major support potential. All red-light companies – of which only the largest charities will have more than a dozen on their list – are maintained as active, current prospects. An amber light indicates that an approach may be made only after discussion and prior approval, thereby ensuring that only the best case for support is presented. Green-light companies are open to any approaches: they are often companies that consider supporting charitable activity only in a very defined geographical area.

The traffic-light system depends on good access to a central database by all corporate fundraisers, and consistent use of it. Fundraisers need to know that they will receive a response on 'amber' companies within a fixed time period. And, in general, any system will work only if there is trust and transparency between all parties, if flexibility is built into the system and if there is clear direction from fundraising management. Only then can all parties feel that they are being dealt with fairly and that the achievement of their fundraising target is not being jeopardised by other colleagues' determination to meet theirs. Trust and transparency mean bringing people together so that they can get to know each other and talk through any issues of dispute.

Also to be built into the system is some record of who is to be credited with income generated. The simplest system is that any fundraiser can be credited with a 'finder's fee', where the subsequent development of a corporate partnership is taken on by a colleague.

Flexibility is needed to accommodate volunteers who may unintentionally break the rules but whose enthusiasm and corporate connections need nurturing, not denouncing. Many corporate fundraisers successfully tap into the contacts and leadership of their trustees, chief executive and other directors, the key to success being these people's willingness to accept the fundraiser's planned relationship building. Some charities have also made good use of business leaders on a 'corporate panel'. Others have found that such panels can take more time to service than is warranted by their resulting contribution. Corporate fundraising systems must also meet legal requirements. That means that many charities will need to have a trading company to handle 'commercial support' from companies. Directors of that company can be drawn from outside the charity as well as from within and so can be a useful way of involving some business leaders.

## Evaluating and reviewing structure

Successful fundraising has to be responsive to a changing world – changing needs that charities seek to meet, and changing attitudes to giving. Nowhere is this more true than corporate giving, where there is often a direct link between profit levels and charitable support. Any structure for corporate fundraising must therefore be kept under constant review. Although this should happen on a cyclical basis and as part of an overall fundraising strategy, it must also be subject to change at short notice when circumstances dictate. Three such examples might be: when a trend for companies to devolve charitable support from the centre to regional offices is identified – which would require charities to change their structure correspondingly in order to maximise potential income from such companies; where there is a shift from sponsorship support to employee involvement in charitable giving; where a change in attitude, driven by potential market-share advantage as a result of an 'ethical stance', may also demand a review of corporate fundraising structure.

# Conclusion

Companies receive many more requests for support than they can meet. They may need to find reason to favour one request over another when there is little to choose between the charity submissions. The experiences illustrated in this chapter show that, where insufficient attention has been paid to structuring corporate fundraising correctly, it undermines the effectiveness of the charity's case: data will be insufficiently captured and shared; fundraisers in different parts of the charity may unwittingly compete against each other in approaches to the same companies.

# CHAPTER EIGHT

# Ethics and standards

**Valerie Morton**

# Introduction

By the very nature of the voluntary sector, ethics and standards have significance for all fundraisers, but they are especially important for corporate fundraisers, both because of the need to balance the objectives of the charity and the corporate partner, and also because of the highly public nature of many such partnerships.

Ask fundraisers what they mean by the term 'ethics' and you are likely to get the 'Heinz' response – 57 different varieties. To ensure full coverage of the subject, this chapter addresses any issue concerning standards and morals that has an impact on corporate fundraisers (for the sake of simplicity, the term 'ethics' will be used to cover all the issues).

A number of the views outlined in the chapter are simply good management practice (in some cases, legal requirements), but some readers may find the approach taken insufficiently 'strict', whereas others may find it too pragmatic. Given the breadth of the voluntary sector, and the nature of each individual's personal convictions, this is hardly surprising and serves simply to reinforce the fact that the subject is likely to generate lively discussion.

The issue of ethical investment has, until recently, been more widely documented than that of ethical fundraising, and some readers may benefit from policies already agreed with regard to investment. Information sources such as EIRIS (Ethical Investment Research Service) can also be useful to fundraisers.

# The relevance of ethical issues to corporate fund-raising

There are two opposite reactions to the complicated subject of ethics, which may be characterised as the 'head in the sand' solution (i.e. just carry on as normal and hope that no one will notice what is going on) and the 'head above the parapet' principle (i.e. be completely open about what you are doing, and accept the risks that go with it). It is easy to apply the 'head in the sand' solution, especially when fundraising targets are at stake, but there are many reasons why the 'head above the parapet' principle is not only right, but also cost effective.

Until recently, consideration of ethical issues relating to corporate fundraising was invariably led by charities. However, the emergence of corporate social responsibility (CSR) as a key priority for so many companies (see Chapter 2) has shifted the balance. It is now often the case that companies look to charities to help them address the ethical element of their CSR strategy, and this has made it even more important that corporate fundraisers take a proactive approach.

Benefits to be gained by developing an ethical policy for corporate fundraising include:

- Generating as much income as possible for your cause by both avoiding loss of income (which might happen if, for example, a deal backfired because of the response of either the public or your charity's stakeholders) and also generating new income (e.g. donors might come forward because of your ethical stance). In addition, having a clear ethical policy will simplify the process of targeting potential corporate supporters, thus improving cost effectiveness.

- Ensuring your charity's values are upheld. Charities fundraise only to fund the cause they exist to support: fundraising is not an end in itself. It is therefore not only counter-productive, but also inappropriate, for a fundraising project to contradict the values of your charity. The Royal National Institute for the Blind (RNIB), for example, with its clear service objective to reduce discrimination against people who are blind or partially sighted, would not consider entering a partnership that might result in the portrayal of a negative image of blind people. A charity whose objectives include saving tropical rainforests would not enter into a promotion to sell hardwood furniture that used timber from endangered forests. The answer is generally, however, not so simple, so the Institute of Fundraising guidance note on 'The acceptance and refusal of voluntary donations' (quoted later in this chapter) is particularly useful.

- Avoiding misunderstanding with potential and active corporate partners. It is unlikely that any fundraiser wants to have to return a donation or refuse an offer of support – a clear, well-publicised policy should prevent such situations arising.

- Fulfilling a responsibility to the sector as a whole. Although corporate partners, and in most cases the public, recognise that each charity is a discrete entity, there is nevertheless a tendency to view charities as a whole, and to ascribe to them certain common characteristics and methods of operation. The activities of one charity can therefore have an effect on the whole sector. A clear policy, reflecting all issues to do with morals and standards, will avoid 'queering the pitch' for other charities.

# Defining the issue

Before you devise your ethical policy for corporate fundraising, you need to define the issue by clarifying the subjects that will be within the scope of that policy. You may wish to keep things simple and confine yourself to one key issue (e.g. the acceptance or refusal of voluntary donations), or you may choose to address the whole range of issues. However, the greater the scope, the more difficult it will be to reach consensus on the subjects covered.

In order to identify the issues you wish to cover in your policy, it may be helpful to consider three areas:

## The company

- general compatibility with your cause
- nature of products or services
- employment practices
- quality standards
- environmental policy and practices
- approach to CSR

## The fundraising mechanism

- adherence to law/industry guidelines
- nature of mechanic (e.g. lottery, affinity product)
- associated products (source, safety, etc.)
- cost effectiveness (e.g. the percentage of income generated going to your cause)

## Background and organisational issues

- minimum guaranteed donation
- promotional methods
- use of the donation (e.g. is it for agreed/budgeted work?).

# Devising an ethical policy for corporate fund-raising

The model that follows shows the eight stages that need to be undertaken when devising and implementing an ethical policy. These stages are:

- research and consultation
- defining the issues relevant to your charity
- creating the policy
- defining procedures
- identifying and creating resources
- implementation – internal and external
- monitoring and evaluating
- revision.

## Research and consultation

### Stakeholders

Much of the research process has the benefit of both finding out facts and also achieving the important task of consultation. Many of your stakeholders will feel it appropriate to express their views. The information they provide will be valuable; equally important, implementation is more likely to be achieved painlessly if stakeholders have been consulted.

Many charities have a broad range of stakeholders:

- service users/beneficiaries
- intermediaries to the above
- trustees
- individual donors
- corporate/trust/organisation donors
- members

- volunteers
- staff
- purchasers
- suppliers.

It is not unusual for different stakeholders, whether in the same 'category' or not, to have very different views. How are these differing views to be reconciled? Differences between beneficiaries are particularly difficult to address: a charity for disabled people may have some beneficiaries who are willing to support any corporate partnership that raises money because of the use to which those funds could be put, whereas others may not support high-profile money-raising partnerships because they rely on a 'sympathy vote' for disabled people that runs counter to any objective of empowerment. The only solution is to ensure the consultation process is carried out as thoroughly as possible, and, equally important, that the decision-making process is seen to be clear and fair.

### External consultation

In addition to researching external stakeholders (in this case, of course, corporate partners are particularly important), it is valuable to consult any relevant trade association of industry bodies: not only will their input be valuable, but their involvement could enhance the external implementation process. The Royal Society for the Protection of Birds (RSPB), for example, when defining their Environmental Policy for Business Partnerships, consulted the CBI's Environmental Business Forum and the International Chambers of Commerce Business Charter of Sustainable Development (see Chapter 13 for a detailed account of this process, pp. 117–21).

## Defining the issues relevant to your charity

There is an argument for defining the issues relevant to your charity before undertaking the research and consultation process. However, until research has been completed, it is difficult to predict the issues that stakeholders feel are relevant. The solution clearly is to outline the issues in advance, but to refine them with the benefit of the research and consultation. The definition of issues set out above (see p. 75) can be used to define a list of the circumstances you wish your policy to cover, some of which are likely to be particular to your charity (e.g. a charity representing children may not consider it appropriate to include environmental issues unless these have a direct impact on children).

# Creating the policy

Creating the policy is arguably the most difficult element of the whole process, because it actually requires making clear decisions. Some of the questions you may need to answer include:

- From which companies, or types of company, will you accept donations? And from which companies, or types of company, will you refuse donations ?

- In what circumstances will you accept/refuse donations?

- Are there any fundraising mechanics you will not undertake (e.g. lotteries, credit cards)?

- Will you always request a minimum donation when undertaking a partnership activity, and, if so, how is this to be calculated?

- Will you require projects to produce income at a certain cost ratio?

- Will you accept funds only for charitable work that has been previously approved, or will you carry out new work if funds are available for that specific purpose only?

It is at this point that personal views can easily come into play. However, it is important that everyone concerned with the process understands their responsibilities in law. This applies in particular to the acceptance and refusal of donations. Charity Commission Leaflet CC3, *Responsibilities of Charity Trustees*, states that 'Trustees must act reasonably and prudently in all matters relating to the charity and must always bear in mind the interests of the charity. They should not let personal views or prejudices affect their conduct as trustees.' It is often difficult for staff, who may hold passionate personal views about various issues, to accept that these views have to be put aside and should not interfere with their fundraising activity. For a more detailed exposition of the legal context to corporate fundraising, see Appendix 1 (pp. 149–66).

As an illustration of this point, a number of years ago the NSPCC was offered a promotion involving the sale of fur coats. Many staff felt uncomfortable with the idea and wanted to turn down the offer, some citing their view that the killing of animals for their fur could encourage cruelty to children. However, the corporate decision was to go ahead. Interestingly, although the charity did receive a number of letters of concern from the public, many of these included a donation, because the people writing them understood that the promotion was being carried out because funds were needed.

# Defining procedures

No matter how good your policy is, it will fail if procedures are not clear and easy to carry out. The issues you may need to consider here include:

- Who will carry out research on companies, and how will this be done? Research may need to be proactive – and influence the decision of which companies to approach – or reactive – and follow the receipt of, or offer of, support. It is also useful to define the nature of the research required (e.g. whether it relates to products, employment practices, etc.).

- What level of delegated authority do staff have? In which circumstances may they make a decision (because that circumstance is clearly set out in the policy), and when do they need to consult management/trustees? The ICFM guidance note suggests that 'procedures for the delegation of decision making should be established in writing and agreed formally by the trustees'.

- What will the ongoing decision-making process be? Will a committee be created? If so, who should its members be?

# Indentifying and creating resources

It is often tempting to believe (and hope) that an ethical policy for corporate fundraising can be created with existing resources. Although staff time may be available for preparing the policy, there are a number of activities that will require a specific resource allocation, for example the research and consultation process, implementation, any ongoing requirement for research, and the evaluation process.

# Implementation – internal and external

Once policy and procedures have been agreed, it is easy to think that the main task has been completed. However, without effective implementation, the policy is useless. Similarly, sending a memo with reams of lengthy script and numerous proformas is a sure way to halt the policy's progress (and alienate the very staff who need to use the procedures). You should devise a promotional campaign worthy of the launch of any new product. Your charity's stakeholders are obvious key internal audiences but, if you are to obtain maximum benefit, external audiences such as potential corporate partners and trade bodies should be included in your campaign.

## Monitoring and evaluating

Monitoring the policy will not only help you to refine it, but it will also support the implementation process. A policy document is far more likely to be read by staff if their views are genuinely being canvassed. Monitoring should be carried out at two stages: shortly after the implementation, to ensure that the policy is clear and understood; and some months later, to discover whether the procedures work in practice. Although it may be stating the obvious, canvass opinion at all levels so that the information is accurate and not just based on what some people think is the case.

## Revision

Some revisions may be necessary immediately following the initial launch of the policy. With luck these will be minor, but an initial revision should be considered after the first full year of use, followed by more detailed ones at intervals of two years.

# Conclusion

The difficult and sensitive nature of ethics and standards can easily become a barrier to creating a policy for ethical corporate fundraising. However, it is important that all good fundraising managers ensure their charity has such a policy. Not only will it facilitate a consistency of approach, but it will also ensure adherence to legal requirements.

# Case histories – the charity perspective

# CHAPTER NINE

# Mencap and Transco – the Safety Charity Challenge

**Rachel Billsberry-Grass**

## Introduction

The Transco and Mencap partnership on the Safety Charity Challenge is a great example of a company and a charity working together for mutual gain. The project took an original and innovative approach to a very real business issue for Transco, and the key reason for its success was, in all likelihood, Transco's commitment to the initiative from the top down – and, of course, the support and added value that the Mencap team was able to bring. The initiative continues to be successful, because very tangible benefits can be seen for both partners.

## The roots of the Safety Charity Challenge

Transco is Britain's major gas pipeline transporter and guardian of the country's gas emergency service. Naturally therefore, safety is its number one priority, both for the public and for its 14,000-plus employees.

The company aspires to an injury-free working environment, and its dedicated health, safety and environment department runs an ongoing high-profile information campaign to educate and constantly remind employees to be vigilant about their own and colleagues' safety. Despite this, accidents at work and the subsequent level of time off due to injury (lost-time injuries) were still too high. In 1999, the company realised that a different approach was needed: this is what led to the creation of the Safety Charity Challenge.

The Challenge was designed as a simple way of aligning the enthusiasm for philanthropy that Transco employees had consistently shown in the past with Transco's core safety objectives. Employees would be asked to identify, report and remove hazards that could lead to lost-time injuries. For every hazard spotted and removed the company would make a charity donation.

Transco's business aims for the challenge were to raise employees' awareness of health and safety in the workplace; to increase the number of hazards spotted; and to reduce the number of lost-time injuries.

## How Transco chose Mencap

Having decided that the Safety Charity Challenge would be the best way to meet its health and safety objectives, the company gave a great deal of consideration to which charity it should work with. Knowing that employees were the key to the success of the campaign, nominations were invited from staff, and many suggestions received. Because it was going to be difficult to estimate how much money would be raised, it was decided that it would be preferable to work with a single national charity rather than spread the money more thinly across a number of different organisations. Three further criteria were applied to narrow down the list of charities, which were that potential partners needed to:

- be well known
- have strong community links
- have the resources and networks needed to work with the company on the Challenge.

It is hard to describe the enthusiasm with which Mencap greeted the call from Transco – although any fundraiser can probably imagine it. Initially Transco made contact with us to chat through the idea. Understandably, the company wanted to avoid raising our hopes, but I was told that it was seriously considering Mencap as a potential partner for an initiative that could be worth around £1 million. I talked through how Mencap met Transco's criteria and about our previous experience of working with large national organisations, in particular as Tesco's 'charity of the year' a couple of years earlier. I followed this up in writing, as requested, with information about Mencap and some suggestions on how we felt that we could add value to the project.

Here I took the lead from my conversation with Transco, picking out the areas that seemed most important. Given that the charity angle was being used as the key motivator for employees, I stressed that we were able to spend the money locally on Mencap's network of community support teams and would provide lots of information – real stories about real people that Transco staff would be helping.

We could also provide PR support in promoting these stories and the Challenge, internally for both organisations and also externally. We would provide named members of staff to work with Transco, nationally and regionally. Mencap has a national network of local societies and, where possible, we would link them with their nearest Transco site. I assured Transco that we would provide support and updates, that we would attend and organise regular review meetings, ensure that Dennis the Menace – our mascot – was available if necessary, and really do anything else they wanted!

From our conversation, I had gathered that Transco was keen to reassure itself that Mencap would be able to deal with what it hoped was to be a major partnership. It was a good opportunity to promote our credentials and talk about some of the companies with whom we had worked recently, including Tesco and Dixons.

Transco greeted this written proposal positively, and it was agreed in principle that we would work together. Before the final commitment a meeting was arranged between key people from both organisations, including senior directors and, importantly, the people who would be working on the project on a day-to-day basis. On Mencap's side, this included myself (I was to oversee the project), Jennifer Dyer (project manager) and Jane Redman (project co-ordinator), both of whom took on increasingly involved roles as the relationship developed. Transco was represented by staff from the health, safety and environment department.

In theory the result of the meeting was a foregone conclusion, but Transco was keen to tell us about the Challenge and get our commitment, and to reassure itself that Mencap was capable of delivering the partnership it expected. Transco was particularly interested in discussing our previous experience of working with other large companies: how we had liaised with them, how we had spent the money raised and how we had kept regionally based people aware of what was happening and motivated to support us.

So it was agreed: Mencap was Transco's chosen charity for the Safety Charity Challenge. At Mencap we ran round the office cheering and waving our arms in the air.

# Planning the challenge

Having agreed to work together in July/August 1999, we had to fly straight into action to be ready for the launch of the challenge at the beginning of September 1999.

Working closely with Transco's representatives, we developed a plan for working together.

The first thing was to agree aims for the Challenge. As I have said, for Transco the overall aim was to increase internal recognition of health and safety, increase the number of hazards spotted, and consequently decrease the number of lost-time injuries. For Mencap the aim was to generate significant funds – at least £500,000.

At this early stage, Transco was slightly wary about agreeing targets. We agreed that our target would not be published at the beginning of the Challenge, but that Transco would underwrite a donation to Mencap of £100,000 – which seemed fair enough.

We also set about drawing up a contract, which included the details of the Challenge and what was expected of each party in the course of the Challenge, including general logistics such as identifying the main contact points in each organisation. We paired Mencap regional staff with the appropriate Transco regions and began to make contacts and develop template presentations.

Materials were produced to add to those general materials that Transco had already produced to promote the Challenge (these included a video and a leaflet, and templates for staff briefings). We arranged for an open letter from our chairman to be printed in the Transco health and safety magazine that was to be distributed to the home address of all Transco staff. The Mencap team also prepared a leaflet that was inserted in the magazine.

To motivate Transco staff we needed to use real stories, so we involved our services staff in finding these – which further spread knowledge of the partnership throughout Mencap.

We gave some thought to how we could provide incentives and tangible links to our cause. We designed a scheme of Bronze, Silver and Gold certificates to be awarded each time a Transco region raised a particular target amount for Mencap. We also linked the amount raised directly with what it would be paying for. For each hazard spotted a donation of around £50 was made – the cost of providing two hours of support to a family.

Together we did some general internal publicity work – a photo shoot with the Transco managing director and Dennis the Menace – which was featured in each partner's internal magazine.

And, finally, we agreed the way in which the core team would liaise: it was decided we should have monthly meetings with regular phone calls in between. Both Transco and Mencap would be responsible for preparing monthly reports to be distributed to all the relevant people to ensure that everyone was up to date on progress and could see particular successes or problems as they happened.

# Getting and keeping the ball rolling

Having sorted out all our plans, the Challenge was launched to Transco staff at the beginning of September. Mencap's regional team started attending health and safety meetings to tell people about Mencap and its involvement with the Challenge. Jane, Jen and I took to stopping the drivers of Transco vans in the street to make sure they knew about the Challenge – an initiative I wouldn't necessarily recommend, as some drivers found it slightly alarming! (We deliberately stopped short of placing hazards in the way of Transco employees, although this was a strategy that we had at the back of our minds had things not gone as well as expected.)

Monthly updates for Transco regions that detailed the number of hazards spotted, the lost-time injuries, the amount raised and awards won, were regularly e-mailed to staff and additionally featured in internal publications.

The Challenge was going very well, and monthly donations of approximately £60,000–£70,000 were rolling in, but inevitably the initial enthusiasm started to die down. The monthly reports clearly showed that there was decreasing activity, and so at the six-month mark we decided to review the project and attempt to inject some more enthusiasm.

This process identified two main reasons for the abatement of enthusiasm and activity: first, people found that the hazard forms that had to be filled in were rather complicated; second, there were still lots of people in Transco who did not know about Mencap.

We decided to produce a video that linked the two organisations and showed some wonderfully motivating stories of families that Mencap was able to support as the result of its partnership with Transco. This was shown at staff meetings, or on loops in canteens and at the Transco site receptions.

A series of open days were organised, which all staff in a region were encouraged to attend. A session on filling in the (newly simplified) forms was held, which was also an opportunity for Mencap to present its message again – so we tried to ensure that these were attended by service deliverers as well as fundraisers.

We decided to use some personal incentives and offered a national competition for the individuals spotting the highest number of hazards in each region. Winners were invited to lunch at the House of

Lords with Lord Rix, Mencap's president. On a smaller scale, monthly incentives such as cinema tickets were offered within a region to those spotting the most hazards.

We had to think creatively about how we could reach Transco staff because the majority of them were out on the road. The idea of sending a mobile-phone text message was eventually rejected for being too complicated. Instead, we produced an audiotape featuring the TV presenter Mary Nightingale talking about a family that she knows whom Mencap has helped. This was stuck on the front of Transco's latest health and safety magazine with an attractive tape cover, and we hoped the package would encourage people to play it in their vehicles as they were travelling around.

In all this activity we used specific regional case studies that were relevant to that particular Transco region, as it was vital that Transco staff understood that the money they raised was being spent locally.

# Results, evaluation and celebration

Monitoring such a huge project was of obvious importance, given the major investment in time and money from both Mencap and Transco. Monthly updates and meetings, plus regular ad-hoc contacts with those working in the field, proved successful and we were able to pass on examples of best practice and to identify and deal with any problems (e.g. reduced participation) very quickly.

We were also able to compare year-on-year results, because Transco kept annual records of hazard spotting and lost-time injuries. Financially we could see that the monthly income put us well on our way to achieving our targets.

By the end of the year, £756,500 had been raised for Mencap. In total, 9,000 hazards had been spotted and removed – against a target of 2,800 – and lost-time injuries had decreased by 21 per cent on the previous year. The challenge had also had a positive effect on employees' knowledge of health and safety and on their employer's approach to it. In a MORI poll, all health and safety questions had an increased approval rating on the same questions two years earlier: for example, 88 per cent of staff answered positively to the statement 'I understand my health and safety responsibilities'.

To celebrate these successes, together we organised a day out at London Zoo, followed by a trip on the London Eye, for representatives of Transco staff from each region, some Mencap families, and senior executives from each organisation. Denise Lewis attended, fresh from her Olympic gold-medal win in Sydney, and we secured lots of publicity, including a great photo in *The Times*.

## Any problems?

When a project has been so successful for both partners it is difficult to look objectively at how things might have been done differently. We did, indeed, have some suggestions for fine tuning, but lots of the 'problems' that occurred (e.g. if a Transco region was found to be under-performing) were dealt with along the way.

It would, however, have been great to have had longer lead times to get things ready. The launch of the Challenge followed so tightly on Mencap being chosen that there was little time to prepare. This in turn meant that some contact with regional Transco sites was delayed and some opportunities missed (e.g. attendance at meetings planned in early September). However, this was not a huge problem in the grand scheme of things – and, frankly, the short notice meant that, mid-year, we could look at an additional £300,000–£400,000 coming into the current budget – how often does *that* happen?

From Mencap's point of view, a fundraising restructure in the middle of the Challenge resulted in a reduction in the size of our regional team. Although we managed to ensure that fundraising staff were available to deal with all Transco regions, there were inevitably some temporary gaps in support. This did not turn into a major problem, but with better planning it could have been avoided.

# The future of the challenge

It was hard to argue with the facts that showed how successful the Challenge had been, and, in the process of our review, we managed to persuade Transco to work with us for a further year.

We were keen to promote the success of the Challenge more widely in both industry sectors, so we entered it for a number of awards. We were all delighted when the Challenge won the 2001 Utility Week Award for Investment in People, the 2001 Institute of Fundraising & Professional Fundraising award for Most Effective Corporate Fundraising Campaign, and was shortlisted for a 2001 BitC Award for Excellence.

# CHAPTER TEN

# Diabetes UK – a case study

**Karen Addington**

## Diabetes UK

Diabetes UK is the charity for people with diabetes. Formerly called British Diabetic Association, it changed its name in May 2000 to reflect its geographical representation, to put 'diabetes' first, and to give it a brand, logo (and modern pink colour) that could begin to compete for public attention with some of the better-known and better-branded charities.

The mission of Diabetes UK is to improve the lives of people with diabetes and to work towards a future where diabetes no longer exists. The charity is committed to this goal through the provision of research, care and campaigning. Each year the charity spends over £4.5 million funding approximately 150 research projects into areas such as the causes and control of diabetes. It operates the Diabetes UK Careline, which offers confidential support and information to people with diabetes and their families on all aspects of living with diabetes. It also campaigns to influence government on issues that affect people with diabetes.

One of Diabetes UK's great strengths, which over the years has enabled it to fight on behalf of people with diabetes, is its mix of members with diabetes and medical members. This mix is still reflected in its structures, its Board of Trustees, and its membership and volunteer committees.

## The fundraising strategy

The new branding of the charity in 2000 helped us to refresh many of our fundraising approaches. Below, the Diabetes UK fundraising director describes the overall fundraising strategy:

*Our fundraising strategy was to optimise the funding opportunities across all available sources of funds, existing and new. Possibly the most dramatic policy change was the shift away from a pure membership focus within the area of individual and family support. To constrain our support constituency thus had been akin to only asking people to support lifeboats if they themselves had been saved by a lifeboat – imagine how tiny the RNLI would be if that were the case!*

*We started to extend our audience for support to those who know people who are affected by diabetes, which was a dramatic shift for us, but still did not maximise our audience. To return to my analogy above, not that many more lifeboats would be funded if you only asked those who know someone who had been saved by a lifeboat. But it did make us feel more like a charity.*

*Our ultimate fundraising strategic goal would be to tap into a level of support from a proportion of the population as a whole which will only be possible with considerably higher, and constant, levels of awareness of the severity of diabetes, which will take many, many years to build. This will be built fastest, and most efficiently, by working in partnership with others, including corporate partners, who will prove critical in funding many of the necessary structural, as well as traditional, frontline charitable activities. It may not be an exaggeration to say that corporate supporters have the potential to make an even bigger contribution to Diabetes UK indirectly through growing our infrastructure, than directly in cash terms.* (Jonathan Parris, Director of Fundraising, Diabetes UK)

# The corporate relations strategy

The underlying objective of our corporate fundraising strategy echoed Jonathan's overall aim to widen the supporter base of the charity. We too tried to widen the types of company that support the charity. Traditionally, Diabetes UK raised considerable amounts of money from companies whose product had a connection to diabetes. We were notoriously bad, however, at raising money from companies that did not have this link. We wanted to compete with the children's and cancer charities for the major corporate Charity of the Year partnerships that are available. We knew how to manage the relationships – we had vast experience of managing such relationships with companies that did have a product link – but companies without the link had not traditionally invited Diabetes UK to pitch with the better-known charities. We knew that we were capable of competing with the more attractive causes. We had a wide appeal that we needed to build upon. After all, there are 2.5 million people in this country with diabetes, and 3 million children living in poverty. The numbers are similar – yet there are dozens of children's charities, and they win many of the highest-profile corporate partnerships. If you were to consider all the people in the UK at risk of developing diabetes – everyone over 40, everyone who is overweight, people from a black or Asian ethnic background, every woman who experienced gestational diabetes during her pregnancy, and everyone with a family history of diabetes – then you are probably talking about a huge proportion of the UK population. Diabetes is just not treated seriously enough, and this was a problem when we were trying to persuade companies to support the charity. We worked to raise awareness of diabetes and of Diabetes UK so that we were able to compete for some of these major partnerships.

We used our corporate relationships to increase the supporter base of the charity in ways that may not immediately seem like corporate fundraising, but nevertheless had a great value to the charity. For example, we used opportunities offered by in-store sampling of healthy food products to capture data of people interested in diabetes. We negotiated with pharmaceutical and medical appliance companies to allow us to send membership or regular-giving recruitment mailings to their databases of customers with diabetes. These activities were targeted and effective, and could not have happened without the support of our corporate partners.

We gradually translated this strategy to widen our corporate supporter base into operational tasks. Diabetes UK began to pitch for major corporate partnerships, for the first time in its history, to companies with no product link to the cause. We won some smaller partnerships and managed them successfully. It will be simply a matter of time, and perhaps a little luck, before diabetes will be the cause on the supermarket carrier bags, or the benefiting charity from the major sporting event.

## Our past success

To return to the areas where we were experienced and successful already, the corporate relations team at Diabetes UK is so called because the charity acknowledged that 'relationships' with our client companies involved much more than simply fundraising. We made wide use of gifts in kind from companies, and our internal accounting procedures were set up so that fundraisers may be acknowledged and rewarded for bringing valuable goods and services into the charity, as well as for raising money. One area where we achieve very valuable gifts in kind is around the sponsorship of our professional conferences. We are able to offer to conference delegates better transport, better meeting facilities, a more professional programme and even better food because companies donate such things from their hospitality budgets, in addition to the donations and sponsorship that they provide to us from marketing and community affairs budgets. In 2001, the corporate relations team made £220,000 worth of gifts in kind available to Diabetes UK. This was a major budgetary achievement, and was reported to the senior management of the charity.

The two commercial sectors where we continue to receive more approaches than we will ever have the resources to deal with are from the pharmaceutical sector and the food and health retail sector. Pharmaceutical products are normally necessary to enable a person living with diabetes to maintain good health, and diet and exercise are key factors in managing the good blood glucose control and weight issues that are so essential to avoiding the serious long-term health problems (such as blindness, heart disease, kidney disease and limb amputations) that uncontrolled diabetes can cause. We won Lloydspharmacy Charity of the Year in 2001; we succeeded in getting a significant proportion of our advertising campaign for 2002 sponsored by a major pharmaceutical company; we won a £100,000 donation to our research programme from Glaxo Wellcome. We were good at working with companies where there is a product link.

This product link made our mixed membership of people with diabetes and diabetes healthcare professionals an ideal target market for information and marketing about these pharmaceutical, food and health products. We understood commercial reality and knew that we were being used to reach people with diabetes and to give a product the implied authority of being associated with the charity that people with diabetes trust. We were comfortable with being able to offer access to people with diabetes for appropriate companies – after all, we exist to help people with diabetes manage their condition, and people need to be informed and aware of appropriate products in order to do this successfully.

However, we recognised our responsibility to provide a balanced view of as many available products as possible and also to verify that any product with which we have associated the charity's name was definitely suitable for the people we represent. We put in place a stringent vetting procedure for the products of any company that wanted to form a fundraising partnership with Diabetes UK.

## The Ethical Working Relationships Policy

We have a comprehensive Ethical Working Relationships Policy agreed by our Board of Trustees, and we are careful to apply the rules of this policy to all new and existing corporate relationships. Diabetes UK offers a copy of this policy on the web site, and we openly discuss the policy with our corporate clients, whenever relevant. Checking all corporate relationships against the policy can result in delays, and has on occasion caused considerable difficulties when an activity proposed by one of our partner companies contravened the policy and was therefore declined. However, if we were to lower our standards, we would risk losing the impartiality that the charity has spent so long building up and we would no longer be the organisation that people with diabetes can trust. The corporate relations team staff work hard to manage the friction between the expectations of our corporate partners and any restrictions imposed by our ethical policy on the 'service' that the charity is able to deliver to these corporate partners. Corporate relations executives have to use tact and diplomacy to keep both sides happy, often when important deadlines may be jeopardised and large amounts of money are at stake.

The members of my team have in the past been treated rather like estate agents both by companies and other charity colleagues. Everybody blamed them, because nobody quite got everything they wanted, exactly how and when they wanted it, even though these charity fundraising 'estate agents' did a great job, kept all aspects of the project together and nearly always pulled off the deal in the end. Unlike estate agents, they received neither commission nor company car for all that effort and diplomacy. I often thought corporate fundraisers were the most undervalued people I knew.

## Team structure

The corporate relations team at Diabetes UK is one of the charity's three fundraising functions. There is also a supporter relations team and a community fundraising team. The corporate relations team is itself split into two teams, each of which has a manager who has income responsibility for the whole team (see Figure 5).

The first of these two teams is the trusts and major gifts team. In addition to raising money from trusts and wealthy individuals, this team also has responsibility for fundraising from events and statutory sources. Much of the events work is City focused, but these skills fit well with our major-gift programme, and our events specialist is largely involved in developing relationships through events with key contacts. There is cross-over here with company fund-raising, and the events help us to recruit new companies as sup-porters. This is an objective of the events fundraiser, although it is sometimes difficult to measure the outcomes as clearly as we would like. As the trusts and major gifts team always meets or exceeds budget and causes no problems, it would be boring to say much more about them, and anyway they are outside the remit of this book.

The second team is the company fundraising team, which has two corporate partnership managers, who each manage corporate rela-tions executives dedicated to a commercial sector. We have a man-ager and an executive who initiate and implement activities with the pharmaceutical sector, an executive responsible for food and health retail sectors, an executive who manages payroll giving and relationships with 'other' companies with no product link to dia-betes, and an executive who deals with sponsorship of our confer-ences and 'other' company fundraising opportunities.

These structures work well because each staff member is able to specialise and become expert in dealing with certain types of com-pany, but also retains all the skills necessary to help out with another commercial sector whenever needed. The whole team can introduce a fundraising event or payroll giving or sponsorship to a corporate partnership, and then rely on the expertise of a colleague to help with implementation.

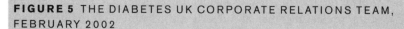

**FIGURE 5** THE DIABETES UK CORPORATE RELATIONS TEAM, FEBRUARY 2002

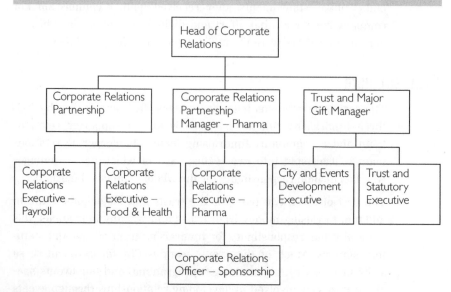

# Key issues affecting success

Many of the challenges that the company fundraising team faced were internal blocks. We were fortunate that our chief executive acknowledged this difficulty and supported us and our colleagues in other departments to remove the blocks to increased corporate fundraising success. This level of senior support was important, as we often asked other departments at Diabetes UK to do work that was not within their own department's operational plan. Colleagues in other departments did not have servicing corporate supporters as their priority, nor even as a key task. We had to remember this while supporting our colleagues to recognise the importance for all charity staff to help to service corporate client relationships if we were to succeed in increasing the level of the charity's corporate income.

An internal block that we effectively removed, thereby enabling us to put together effective fund applications, was the difficulty that fundraisers used to have in obtaining details about the work under-taken by the service departments of the charity. We established a system of a 'project directory' that the whole charity adopted. Every activity undertaken by every department was listed on a summary sheet, together with a page of project details – including costs, tar-get audience, timescales and any existing funding – held in a central computer file. All members of the corporate relations team could access this information. A paper copy was also kept in the office, so that anyone could take a relevant project to a potential funder at a moment's notice.

A major challenge that faced the corporate relations team was to provide an adequate level of PR and media work for corporate sup-porters. We have a dedicated PR and media team at Diabetes UK, but their function is to create PR opportunities for the charity, not for our corporate clients; they also work at full capacity to achieve their own PR objectives. The corporate team regularly tried to pull the PR and media team away from their core work to raise the pro-file of our corporate partnerships. This was an internal challenge that we all faced and worked together to solve.

Another key issue to affect success that Diabetes UK addressed and resolved was the involvement of senior staff and trustees in corpor-ate fundraising work. We have the full support of our entire senior management team for the corporate relations function. The senior staff, and several trustees, submitted to training in major donor work. They all make their time available to the corporate team for presentations to companies and generously pass over any corporate contacts they make in the course of their work when they think that the corporate relations team could develop a relationship into a more financially profitable one for the charity. This enables us to avoid any dual approaches to companies, or individual contacts, and to make the best use of the skills and experience of the corporate relations team to maximise income for the charity. It is a valuable resource to the corporate relations team.

The key to the corporate fundraising success of any charity like Diabetes UK, a medium-sized charity without the benefit of a strong brand like the NSPCC, is the quality of its corporate fundraising staff. Their ability to build effective relationships for the charity and then to deliver what the company wants from the partnership is the only way that we can compete at the same level as the bigger charities. The corporate team at Diabetes UK achieves a cost-to-income ratio of about 1:3 overall, which is pretty good compared with similar-sized charities.

Over the last few years of implementing this strategy, the corporate relations team has grown in confidence and begun to see itself more as an equal partner to companies, rather than as an inferior supplicant. We saw that we could offer real marketing benefits to companies and began to value ourselves accordingly.

# A case study – Benecol

This case study of one of our successful corporate partnerships is an excellent example of a charity–corporate relationship where both parties benefited from the association.

Benecol is a range of foods that are proven to reduce LDL (bad cholesterol) by up to 14 per cent when eaten as part of a healthy diet.

Our relationship with Benecol began when their PR company, Hill & Knowlton Public Relations Counsel, approached us in February 2001 because they wanted to support a relevant charity. Fortunately we were able to deliver a sufficient number of promotional opportunities almost immediately and to tie the activities in with our existing National Diabetes Week in June 2001.

Benecol supported Diabetes UK in several ways.

## A win–win magazine sponsorship

They sponsored a magazine that featured information on cardiovascular health and was mailed to our database of 210,000 members. The subject matter of the magazine was relevant to the Benecol range of foods, since these have been proven to reduce cholesterol. The link between cholesterol and coronary heart disease (CHD) is well established: for every 1 per cent reduction in cholesterol people may reduce their risk of CHD by 1 to 2 per cent. People with diabetes are at an increased risk of heart disease, particularly mature people with type 2 diabetes, and these people make up the majority of our members.

Benecol's support for this project went beyond merely sponsoring the costs of the magazine. They also offered editorial for the magazine, advice from a state-registered dietician, radio interviews during National Diabetes Week with a top heart expert, and a recipe from celebrity chef Antony Worrall Thompson.

The final outcome of the project was entirely successful, although its implementation was not all plain sailing: for example, there was some miscommunication as we tried to get other internal teams involved. The main lesson we learned was that a client should ideally have just one point of contact with the charity, and this person must keep all other internal staff completely informed of any issues arising. However, we established a good working relationship, far removed from the 'estate agent' model mentioned before!

This said, the sponsorship and the magazine were a resounding success. Benecol was able to raise brand awareness with their target market, and Diabetes UK was able to produce a specialist magazine offering essential health advice to people with diabetes. This was a real win–win.

## Web site link

The Diabetes UK web site is an authoritative source of information about managing diabetes, and several companies buy a time-limited web link to the Diabetes UK web site. Benecol set up a link to our site on the much-visited 'healthy eating' pages, and this link was available over the National Diabetes Week period.

## T4D

T4D is a community fundraising initiative, based on the National Diabetes Week campaign, which aims to raise awareness of diabetes through a simple fundraising technique of asking organisations and individuals to hold a tea party. It also helps to dispel the myth that people with diabetes cannot eat sugary foods such as cakes and biscuits. There is a T4D pack, which has recipes, a quiz, fun ideas for adults and children and general facts about diabetes. The marketing of the campaign is based on *Balance*, which is sent to 210,000 members of Diabetes UK and to clubs and organisations whose membership fits a 45-plus age profile. This initiative is also mentioned on the Diabetes UK web site.

Benecol part-sponsored these marketing materials, and again raised brand awareness with their target audience. Benecol inserted an Antony Worrall Thompson recipe, a voucher to obtain a free snack bar, and an information leaflet entitled 'Reducing your cholesterol level with Benecol foods'. A reminder postcard was sent to those people who have been slow to send in their sponsorship money. The Benecol logo was on each postcard.

### 'Are you at risk?' – Risk Factor Flyer

Benecol sponsored the diabetes awareness leaflet that was sent out during National Diabetes Week to inform people about the risks of diabetes:

- 147,000 were sent out to health-care professionals and GP surgeries;
- 120,000 were sent out in response to the advertising billboards;
- the remainder were mailed to all who request information from the charity.

### Sampling opportunities

Finally, we offered Benecol the opportunity to provide samples at our Annual General Meeting and at a Living With Diabetes Day conference. These meetings were well attended by people with diabetes and enabled Benecol to reach people who would benefit from their foods directly.

This corporate relationship was a good example of how fundraising can provide a company with the methods of achieving their own publicity objectives. Given the tight timetable for the sponsored activities with this company, Diabetes UK, Benecol and Hill & Knowlton managed a remarkable number of projects with excellent outcomes.

We hope that you will see more corporate partnerships from Diabetes UK that are as successful as this one in the future.

# CHAPTER ELEVEN

# Cause-related marketing from the NSPCC

**Annabel James**

## The effect of the FULL STOP campaign

The NSPCC's FULL STOP campaign has been one of the most high-profile campaigning and fundraising initiatives ever launched for a social cause.

The extraordinary public awareness following the launch of our 1999 advertising campaign translated into reality, generating more money than ever before for the charity (£100 million to date), demonstrably raising awareness of the issues of child abuse and neglect and, most crucially, increasing the amount that the NSPCC was able to spend on service provision for children across the UK by more than 10 per cent from one year to the next.

The strength of the NSPCC FULL STOP brand is the currency the NSPCC is now able to leverage to continue its fundraising drive and campaigning stance. Research carried out by the independent think-tank the Future Foundation in January 2001 confirmed the NSPCC as the most-effective campaigning organisation among UK MPs. This, coupled with the highest spontaneous consumer awareness among all charities at 42 per cent (an increase of 12 per cent), gives the NSPCC real firepower in pursuing its aim of ending cruelty to children.

The NSPCC's challenges now and in the future are to use this extraordinary backdrop of awareness and success to broaden the base of the campaign and, ultimately, to move response to FULL STOP from awareness, through responsibility, to action. To this end, campaigning and fundraising are inextricably linked, and, from an NSPCC perspective, cause-related marketing (CRM) initiatives are the means to do this.

# How to define CRM?

Like other charities perhaps, the NSPCC is unclear about the exact definition of CRM. There is a kaleidoscope of buzzwords bandied about by both charities and corporates, and we are constantly struggling to understand what potential supporters mean by 'corporate social responsibility (CSR)', 'corporate community involvement (CCI)' and 'cause-related marketing'. Just as the first becomes more widely recognised, the second appears to be becoming a catch-all expression, and the third, the subject of this chapter, seems sometimes to be used to encompass the other two, and sometimes as a separate part of the marketing mix.

Our confusion derives from whether linking a brand with a cause is a means to an end (and thus part of a larger agenda) or an end in itself. Of course, it doesn't matter *per se*: whether we're engaged in an initiative that bears all the hallmarks of a broad CSR programme, or something that at face value is short term, tactical and largely product driven, the principles are, if not the same, then certainly similar. It is the practical application that differs, and the challenges presented by each different permutation.

From an NSPCC perspective, Gordon Storey, head of external affairs of Masterfoods (formerly Mars Confectionery), a long-term partner of the NSPCC, summed up the essence of our position when he said:

*The benefits that can be delivered through an integrated and strategic partnership are extensive. The power of brands to communicate with consumers is strong. In order to be successful, cause-related marketing should be more than on-pack promotion, and activities will require support from across the organisation. Tangible results in terms of sales will always be important, but the benefits to corporate brand image must not be underestimated.*

The NSPCC has found that, although the same broad principles apply to all corporate–charity links, there are differences in focus between technique-driven, transactional product promotion initiatives, and integrated, holistic corporate partnerships. The two are not mutually exclusive, and the rules for success are similar in both cases, but the corporate's objectives behind the particular initiative ultimately drive the process and inevitably the results.

First, let's deal with the NSPCC's objectives, which do not change whoever we do business with and which underpin our approach when working with companies. These are:

- raising money

- raising awareness of FULL STOP and the work that is done, and needs to be done, to bring about an end to cruelty to children

- delivering tangible and measurable results for our partners to deliver real business benefits.

These are the starting points for the NSPCC and the filters we apply at each stage in the process of developing a relationship with a corporate.

This chapter looks at two case studies that both focus on tactical promotions, CRM initiatives in their simplest and, arguably, purest forms. The results of each are similar in some respects: they were both successful, but they were successful for the corporate for entirely different reasons. When understood together, it is to be hoped that they will demonstrate most accurately the problems the NSPCC has faced in ensuring we deliver successful CRM initiatives, however the term is defined.

# Two disctinctive promotional campaigns with Masterfoods (a division of Mars UK Ltd)

Masterfoods (formerly Mars Confectionery) has committed its support to the NSPCC FULL STOP campaign in myriad ways.

There have been recent on-pack promotions on FUNSIZE and SNICKERS, both of which have been supported by marketing and PR activities. These brand promotions were extended throughout the organisation and related activities incorporated into employee events.

## FUNSIZE 'Share a Smile' promotion

The 'Share a Smile' promotion ran on FUNSIZE. 'Smile' tokens were printed on the back of special packs, and, for every ten collected, Masterfoods donated £2 to the NSPCC. To encourage consumers to purchase, and to build interest over and above the charity link-up, consumers sending in tokens also received a free bag of FUNSIZE.

Masterfoods supported 'Share a Smile' with a national radio campaign made up of a combination of commercial airtime and promotional activity. The advertisements were targeted at mothers aged between 25 and 44, and were followed up with promotional activity run on media partners GWR Group stations. Listeners were invited to call in when they heard 'Share a Smile' comedy clips for the chance to win free FUNSIZE and the grand prize of a family holiday to California. The initiative was supported by promotional trailers and mentions by presenters.

GWR commented:

*'Share a Smile' was a fantastic promotion with a real feel-good factor. During the competition Masterfoods and NSPCC dominated our programming with several 'Share a Smile' comedy clips, which were a really fun addition. The response levels were very high, and the major prize an absolute dream for most kids I know.*

The NSPCC provided PR support by placing competitions in regional newspapers that offered readers the chance to win a year's supply of FUNSIZE. In addition, the NSPCC communicated about the initiative through our extensive regional network of staff and volunteers who, among other initiatives, distributed leaflets to local schools and groups.

## SNICKERS 'Grab Wembley Glory' promotion

SNICKERS also ran a promotion – 'Grab Wembley Glory' – which gave fans the chance to win a piece of football history. This on-pack promotion offered 300 instant-win 'hot spots' of Wembley turf following the demolition of the ground in 2000. In addition, for each 'snacktime' and 'multi-pack' bought, SNICKERS gave 5p to the NSPCC. Again, the promotion incorporated a direct reward to the consumer in addition to the link to the NSPCC. In this case, the NSPCC's added value to the promotion coincided with a specific initiative – Football FULL STOP. This was focused around a weekend of football-related activity, led by the Premier League and consisting of fundraising and awareness activities across football clubs, with support from major broadcasters and football personalities.

While the FUNSIZE and SNICKERS brands were doing their bit, Masterfoods also encouraged employees to become involved by running a special fundraising week. These combined activities have so far raised over £100,000 for the NSPCC, and the partnership is continuing into 2002.

## Assessing the promotions

The key questions of course are: did the promotions meet the criteria of CRM, did we meet the objectives set at the beginning, and what did we learn?

In terms of meeting the CRM criteria, the overall response would be 'Yes'. Masterfoods and NSPCC are mutually compatible brands, at both a corporate and product-brand level.

The approach taken for each promotion was different, since FUN-SIZE and SNICKERS appeal to different segments of the target audiences. The more traditional FUNSIZE product was approached through the target of mums and kids, and SNICKERS through a specific section of the community – those with an interest in football.

A critical lesson for both promotions was the need to reward the consumer beyond the mere feel-good factor of supporting a worthy cause. This is a fundamental point that needs to be considered from the outset – not least because it plays a significant role in the financial planning and modelling before the promotion gets out of the research and development phase.

We needed to understand what each brand required in order to make the final decisions, and this included working out the variable costs, redemption rates, break-even levels and so on. What you need to know will vary according to the brand: the critical factor is to understand that, even though the same principles may apply, the practical application will be different in every case.

The importance of a media partner can also not be overestimated. Leaving aside the obvious point of providing an avenue for promotion, the value this added in terms of raising more general awareness of the NSPCC and of our objectives, while also supporting Masterfoods, was clear.

# Quenching the thirst for thirst pockets

Georgia Pacific is the major manufacturer in the British Isles kitchen towel market, supplying a range of branded and private label products (with an estimated market share of 40 per cent).

In an attempt to protect its overall market position and also to add value, Georgia Pacific developed KittenSoft Thirst Pockets – the thirstiest kitchen towel available. Launched in 1996, the brand was acknowledged by A C Nielsen, in a 1998 fastest-growing brands survey conducted with *Marketing* magazine, to be the UK's fastest-growing brand, with sales up 113 per cent on the previous year.

Towards the end of 1999, Georgia Pacific received confirmation that Procter & Gamble was about to enter the market with its brand, Bounty, and that it would support this with a package valued at more than all the money to be spent on existing brands put together, and more than Bounty would generate in sales in its first year.

What Georgia Pacific required was a means of holding both listings and sales in the face of what appeared to be overwhelming competition. Georgia Pacific needed to do something that would motivate the consumer, would be different and involving – and with a charity link to gain both the retailer's and the public's support.

## 'Design a Kitchen Towel for the Millennium'

KittenSoft Thirst Pockets invited 7–11-year-old children at 6,000 primary schools to take part in a competition to develop a design for a new kitchen towel. This competition, named 'Design a Kitchen Towel for the Millennium', was linked with the NSPCC – an obvious link for a child-orientated promotion. The winning entries were developed into printable designs, to be available for sale. Each printed design included the winner's name and age. The designs were randomly packed, with either two or three rolls per pack, and sold for £1.49.

For every children's millennium competition pack sold, Georgia Pacific made a donation of 10p to the NSPCC. A first, second and third prize was awarded for each of the age categories, W H Smith vouchers of varying values, which could be exchanged by both the winning schools and pupils for books, CDs, videos, etc.

The first-prize winners were also rewarded with a weekend trip to London, where they were presented with their framed designs and gift vouchers at the Rainforest Café.

Almost 600 designs were submitted, and more than 500,000 millennium packs were sold during the promotional period. Press coverage included trades and regional media. Over £60,000 was donated to the NSPCC.

Despite a heavy launch by Procter & Gamble's Bounty, which saw it take a high share of the market shortly after launch, Georgia Pacific saw the sales of Thirst Pockets continue to grow, despite having a marketing budget of one-tenth the size of Bounty's.

The millennium pack promotion was a great success and provided genuine incremental sales that saw Thirst Pockets achieve an all-time high market share during the promotional period. Indeed, the demand for the millennium pack far outstripped both estimates and available stock.

It was not only Georgia Pacific who benefited from this promotion (Thirst Pockets is on course to overtake Bounty and become brand leader), nor the NSPCC, but also the school children who won a prize and their schools.

At the conclusion of the promotion, Steve Duncan, director of brand marketing at Georgia Pacific, said:

*We are delighted with the results of our on-pack promotion with the NSPCC. The association assisted sell-in to the trade as well as excellent sell-through to the consumer. Sales of KittenSoft Thirst Pockets kitchen towel actually doubled through the period of the promotion, and demand outstripped supply.*

## Dixcel Happy Kids project

This activity paved the way for future NSPCC–Georgia Pacific initiatives, and in particular a licensing agreement for the NSPCC Happy Kids, a series of cartoon characters. The association has been extended to include other Georgia Pacific brands, most recently the Dixcel toilet tissue range, which has a whole different series of challenges and objectives, primarily because they do not have the same distribution channels as KittenSoft.

The key objectives of this partnership are primarily to increase sales, and thereby raise funds for the NSPCC. The strength of the association and brand synergy is exploited to the benefit of both the NSPCC and Georgia Pacific. We have included multiple fundraising mechanisms on this product with the prime feature on-pack being the Happy Kids.

Consumers collect on-pack tokens and redeem them for a Happy Kid Doll for the price of £2.99. For each Happy Kid purchased, the NSPCC will receive an additional 50p. This promotion also rewards the company that makes the Happy Kids dolls for the NSPCC, as they have paid a fixed price to the NSPCC for licensing. When the contracted 18 months of the association with Dixcel is fulfilled, the NSPCC will have received the minimum guaranteed amount of £50,000 from the sales of the Dixcel toilet tissue family range.

Once again, we applied the principles from the outset and met the objectives that were set. We learned that a link with a charity is as valuable in Georgia Pacific's own trade negotiations as it is in driving sales and generating income.

# Conclusion

It is the difference in approach between Masterfoods and Georgia Pacific that is the key to understanding the breadth and depth of CRM, however it is defined. Masterfoods has taken a holistic, integrated and genuinely long-term view of its total relationship with the NSPCC. Short-term tactical promotions designed to increase sales are a significant aspect of the relationship. However, Masterfoods' ability to participate in broader initiatives such as Football

FULL STOP (designed to raise awareness of the issue of child abuse among a particular segment of the audience), and to put the whole weight of the company behind it, is a true demonstration of CSR. Georgia Pacific takes a slightly different approach, using the NSPCC relationship much more tactically through branded product promotions – CRM in its original form.

In both cases, however, the results are similar:

- Sales of a branded product are promoted.
- Brand awareness is raised and value added to the brand.
- Retail and consumer PR is generated.
- The company's image of caring for the community is enhanced.

The NSPCC has also been able to meet its own objectives of raising money and awareness and deliver business benefits. The ultimate win–win–win possible, whether you call it CSR, CCI or CRM.

# CHAPTER TWELVE

# Payroll giving

**Louise Anderson**

*NCH is one of the UK's leading children's charities. We work with over 89,000 vulnerable children, young people and their families, through more than 460 projects, to ensure they reach their full potential.*

*375,000 people a month are doing it ...*

*Are you ... ?*

This was just a small part of NCH's strategy to make payroll giving attractive to supporters. Payroll giving had not been part of NCH's fundraising portfolio before 2000, when a strategic review of our fundraising mix, which aimed to increase net income and improve upon our overall cost effectiveness, identified payroll giving as an area of potential in which we should invest.

In fact, in 1992, we had reviewed the income levels attained by other charities promoting payroll giving and recommended that NCH follow suit. However, as often happens in organisations, although the recommendation was approved, there was no systematic promotion of payroll giving, and any income raised was simply through individual enthusiastic fundraisers or supporters.

## Understanding payroll giving

Before looking at NCH's strategy, here is a brief overview of payroll giving, which is essentially a tax-effective form of charitable giving.

An employee commits to make a regular monthly donation from their salary to a charity. Because they do this, the government allows the tax they have paid on that donation to go to their chosen charity. At current tax rates (22 per cent basic rate, 40 per cent higher rate), every £1 donors donate will only 'cost' them 78p (or 60p if they pay higher rate tax – see Table 1). In addition, until 5 April 2003, the government will add an extra 10 per cent to the employee's pledge amount.

**TABLE 1** THE TAX EFFECTIVENESS OF PAYROLL GIVING

| Pledge by donor (gross) | Direct from donor (net @ 22% tax) | Direct from donor (net @ 40% tax) | Value of the donation with 10 per cent government subsidy |
|---|---|---|---|
| £5.00 | £3.90 | £3.00 | £5.50 |
| £10.00 | £7.80 | £6.00 | £11.00 |
| £20.00 | £15.60 | £12.00 | £22.00 |

As a result of this tax element, payroll-giving donations must be processed (and the tax claimed) by an agency charity, which also distributes funds to the causes nominated by staff. Agency charities generally charge a small administration fee.

# Why NCH chose payroll giving

### Internal factors

Overall, payroll giving has great potential for charities and it held two principal attractions for NCH. First, because response rates[1] are well tested and known within the sector, we could build a regular, measurable income base. As it is a form of regular giving, this income could be predicted over a number of years (the average payroll giver is loyal for over five years – see Table 2).

Second, as we already had a well-developed corporate fundraising team, it would be straightforward for us to incorporate payroll giving into our fundraising portfolio without investing in new staff, certainly initially. The amount of good internal and external PR to be gained from the smaller 'investment' can be substantial, and NCH, having dedicated corporate PR officers, was in a good position to maximise this. Similarly, we could integrate a specific communications plan for payroll givers within our overall relationship marketing work.

**TABLE 2** PREDICTED INCOME BASED ON STANDARD KEY PERFORMANCE INDICATORS[1]

| No of staff | Income in first year | Income over five years |
|---|---|---|
| 50 | £1,018 | £4,896 |
| 100 | £2,035 | £9,792 |
| 300 | £6,100 | £29,100 |
| 1000 | £20,300 | £97,600 |

[1]There will obviously be regional variations, based on average salaries/economic conditions in the area.

---

[1] Response rate of 25 per cent; average donation value of £10–12 per month; average donor retention of 5–8 years; likely agency charity administration fee 4 per cent of donation.

We could promote payroll giving as an *easy* way to give for employers. Easy to administer, it is a cost-effective way of 'corporate' giving, as the core money comes from staff rather than from the company[2] itself. Matched giving (where the company donates, for example, the same amount as that raised by staff) can maximise the amount raised, still at less cost to the company.

We were also able to support internal promotional campaigns, which can generate great enthusiasm among staff. For a charity with low brand awareness (as NCH is), payroll giving offered an opportunity to raise individual awareness of our brand within a company.

Finally, the conclusion of our review of NCH's fundraising mix was that we should focus on those areas of fundraising that were both relatively and absolutely cost effective and would reliably raise a high level of net annual voluntary income.

### External reasons

We judged the market to be both growing and supportive.

The voluntary sector received more than £55 million through payroll giving in 2000. This was generated from only 600,000 donors (or 2 per cent of the overall UK workforce), and the bulk of it went to the small handful of charities that have actively promoted payroll giving.

By contrast, 30 million people in the UK are paid through PAYE and are therefore eligible to give through their payroll. Of these, 5 million are already able to give through their payroll, through the 9,000 companies that have already set up (but may not be using) payroll-giving schemes.

Since April 2000, the government has actively promoted payroll giving to companies as part of the Giving Campaign, and now aims to increase payroll giving donations to £60 million a year by 2002/2003.

## Implementing the payroll-giving strategy

Having identified payroll giving as an opportunity, NCH needed to make sure it succeeded. Our previous obstacle had been that the people who needed to deliver the strategy – our corporate fund-

---

[2] Although I have often used 'company' in this chapter, any employer who operates a PAYE system can facilitate payroll giving.

raisers – did not know enough about the scheme and how to promote it.

## Training

Our first step, therefore, was to produce a very comprehensive manual, which we called a tool kit, and to deliver in-depth training to all our corporate and community fundraisers. (This latter was because we wanted to cast our net as wide as possible, and recognised that many of our local fundraisers had links to public-sector bodies or leads through individual supporters who worked in local companies and could be approached.)

The manual and the training covered the basics of payroll giving discussed above, but were also pragmatic and went into considerable detail about how fundraisers could promote the scheme. Fundraisers were given as much opportunity as possible to discuss likely issues, using their current clients as cases in point. We also provided a generic 'pitch' presentation and a general script to use when speaking to employees, which were role played in small groups, and we went through the paperwork involved, to get people used to it.

The aim of all this activity was two-fold: to sell into fundraisers the benefits of adding payroll giving to their portfolio, and to give them confidence that they had everything they needed to ask people to consider giving through their payroll.

Some of the training involved generic advice about the 'pitch' process, to reinforce both pitching skills and also the fact that payroll giving was an easy addition to existing practice. However, other advice covered topics like 'running a successful campaign', 'questions your client might ask (and their answers)', 'objections companies might raise (and how to counter them)' and 'how to target companies successfully'.

## NCH as a case study

NCH already had a payroll-giving scheme, but only a couple of people (one of them the author) out of a staff of almost 5,000 used it, and it had never been promoted to staff.

At the beginning of 2001, key senior staff agreed to begin promoting payroll giving to NCH's own staff. We were very clear that we did not expect staff to give to NCH, but to causes of their own choice. We did, however, feel strongly that we wanted to follow the best practice we recommended ourselves as an employer, and that by this means we would gain credibility – and a good case study – for our conversations with corporates.

Secondary objectives were to give some of our fundraisers practice in promoting payroll giving, and to encourage staff to generate leads into companies through their personal contacts.

The structure of NCH is divided into nine regions and countries, with head offices in Highbury, London; however, the majority of our staff is based in 450 projects across the UK. To speak to everyone face to face was impossible, so we knew we would have to rely on a cascade effect, and support this through central and regional communications. We decided to use Highbury (where about 250 staff are based) as a pilot, and roll out to the rest of the organisation from there.

# The campaign model

We wanted to kick off the promotion in as eye-catching a way as possible and did so by leaving a crème egg on everyone's desk after work on the Tuesday after Easter. Responses ranged from happy tucking in all the way through to outright suspicion (a few people didn't eat theirs in case it left them beholden to an unknown force!). We followed up during that week with cryptic e-mails to all staff and posters around the building.

Moving from a crème egg to payroll giving was a slightly tortuous process, but we made it, changing the e-mails and posters to give more snippets of information every couple of days. The daily menu in the staff canteen was altered to echo themes used in the teaser posters, and staff were mildly disconcerted to find themselves eating the Taxman's Tax-Free Tomato Soup among other things. On the Monday of the following week, all staff received a memo from our chief executive explaining payroll giving, endorsing the promotion, and informing managers that staff champions would be making an appointment to visit their department in the next few days to talk about it. The memo had a payroll-giving form attached.

Staff champions may be enthusiastic members of staff, members of a work charity committee, staff social club, friends or relatives of your charity's staff, or even recently retired employees. The majority of ours were fundraisers, but we managed to recruit some staff from our central support departments as well, so people did not feel overwhelmed by marketers. All non-fundraisers were recruited directly face to face and chosen because of their general popularity and people skills. We wrote a very comprehensive briefing pack for our champions, giving them all the basic information they needed as well as tips for talking to people about payroll giving and a two-minute script they could use if appropriate. The pack had a very strong emphasis on the value of their effort – we calculated that an hour of their time could be worth £480 in total for a charity.

We also put on a lunch for them, which we used as an opportunity for people to talk through any concerns or questions, or just to air nerves! Champions were paired with people from other departments than their own, at their own choice – although you may find some people want to stay within their own teams. We also provided big yellow flowers for people to wear if they felt happy to, so they were easy to identify. (In an external campaign we would have provided NCH T-shirts and so on; since we were not fundraising for NCH, this did not seem appropriate.)

We knew that to gain a good response we had to try to give everyone a chance to talk to someone face to face. The ostensible reason for champions calling on staff was to collect the forms. We asked everyone to hand them back whether they were used or not, so that people were not embarrassed if they did not want to be involved (and because apathy rules and, if you are not proactive, your response rate will be far lower).

Some people had questions, a couple of people wanted in-depth information on the relative merits of payroll giving and Gift Aid (would this only happen in a charity?), and we came back to them on their questions after the event.

## Rolling out the promotion

We also wrote to former employees holding a staff pension, to encourage them to take part. It is not widely known that individuals can generally payroll give through their pension schemes (some pension schemes have been reluctant to provide this service, but can be lobbied by their members – public- and voluntary-sector schemes are generally positive). This was a fairly straightforward process and received positive feedback from people glad to be informed about the scheme.

Covering off the rest of our staff has taken time. All internal communications vehicles have carried articles about payroll giving in the past few months. We have marketing managers based in the regions who act as link roles to our operations department (which employs the vast majority of staff), and they have had full briefings and are operating as champions within their region. All link roles are making joint presentations with the regional HR managers at regional managers' meetings, asking them to carry the key messages and forms back to their projects, to talk through at team meetings. We also now include payroll-giving materials in our induction packs so that all new staff have that information when they start at NCH.

We plan an update in our staff magazine at the end of this year, when we can give a better sense of response nationally to the campaign.

### Follow-up from receiving charities

Anecdotally, colleagues who elected to give to other charities have received a mixed welcome. For our own payroll givers, NCH now has a communications programme designed especially for payroll givers, which is essentially a twice-yearly newsletter. Some charities also run a cash appeal, usually at Christmas, and we have planned an upgrade for 18 months after sign-up. Some of our payroll givers have signed up anonymously, so we have also built in regular communications through their employer.

# And the results are ... ?

In terms of monitoring the success of the initiative, the votes are still coming in, as they say. However, within our central office, payroll giving has increased from 0.04 per cent of staff to 7 per cent – a huge increase. We anticipate a lower response in the regions, given the lack of direct face-to-face contact, but are still confident of an overall increase of between 4 and 5 per cent. This is a lower rate than we would expect (and have begun to get) from an external promotion, but we are nonetheless pleased with the result, not least because our senior managers in particular have passed over some key leads, which we have begun to develop.

## Key learning

For us, the learning has been huge, and we now feel better equipped to promote payroll giving outside NCH. We already have a number of successful pitches, and are beginning to see real money coming in, both from major national promotions, and also from a number of smaller regional promotions. Key hints and tips from these and our own campaign would be:

- In terms of forecasting, don't underestimate the time it can take to develop leads into pitches, and pitches into promotions.
- If the organisation you're working in has a dispersed workforce, be aware that it will take a long time to get to all of them. It's better to

accept this and aim for some element of face-to-face communication, even though it will take longer, as your response rates will be higher.

- Find the right people to sell in the key messages to different groups, and use them as often as possible. Find out which message works best and lead on that. For us, it was 'We are *not* fundraising for NCH' that had to come first.

- Although you should keep the tax and other calculations simple, make sure you have the 'workings out' close to hand so you can prove where your figures are coming from if anyone asks.

- Give people a way of returning their forms anonymously. We collected these in sealed envelopes, and sent them straight to our payroll department. Some people are very keen that their managers do not know whether they're giving in case, for example, it affects their performance review.

- Make sure you understand how the logistics will work even if you're not managing them yourself. We made a point of stressing that giving was private, only to find that our post room had stuck name labels on the forms as they were sent out – which gave a different impression. We had to work hard to overcome this.

- On a related point, you may need to assure the employer before your promotion that you will keep the names and addresses of their staff confidential to your charity; if so, make sure they are flagged appropriately on your database.

- Plan ahead to be able to give people some results, however incomplete. This will keep up momentum and encourage late givers – everyone wants to be associated with success.

- Make friends with the payroll manager. Although it's not huge, your promotion will create some workload for their team and it's wise to have them on your side.

## Conclusion

NCH was thrilled that our payroll-giving promotion to our staff received the Institute of Fundraising/Professional Fundraising Award for Best Payroll Giving Promotion in 2001. However, the real benefits to us have been the lessons we have learned, the leads we have developed, and the awareness we have raised internally of how important payroll giving is to us – and, of course, the impetus to make sure we follow through this particular fundraising strategy, and reap the benefits we have identified.

# CHAPTER THIRTEEN

# Three case studies in ethics and standards

**Valerie Morton and Adrian Penrose**

## Case study 1 – Who pays the promotional costs? Reaching a financial impasse

This case study highlights a number of issues relating to standards and ethics in corporate fundraising. In particular, it demonstrates the responsibility a charity has to ensure partnerships genuinely generate support for the charity, and the need to ensure the public understands the nature and value of that support. (Readers should bear in mind that the situation described arose before the implementation of the Charities Act.)

Charity Y was delighted when it was informed by a PR agency that X, a medium-sized retail company, had selected them to be its Charity of the Year. The news was particularly welcomed because it was the staff of X who had nominated the charity, which suggested that a certain degree of support could be counted on from the staff.

At the initial meeting with the agency and the PR manager from the company, it was explained that the company had adopted charities in the past, but that the goodwill of the staff in the previous year had been lost because a number of promises made by the charity – chief among which had been the promise of celebrity visits to each store – had not materialised. In addition, the company was facing a tough financial situation and was, in effect, hoping to get as many benefits as possible from the new charity partnership without having to employ any pump-priming money. To make matters even more difficult, the company expressed an unwillingness to enter into any activity that could negatively affect profit margins. So, for example, most product promotions were ruled out because it would be impossible to guarantee that margins would remain intact.

Knowing how valuable charity adoptions can be, both financially and in terms of profile generated, the charity was determined to develop some ideas that would enthuse the company. The company's main objectives were to improve profile and develop loyalty by involving the customer, and so the charity suggested organising a record-breaking event: income would be generated by selling a series of promotional badges to customers, with the opportunity for customers also to participate in or observe the record-breaking attempt. As Charity Y had excellent community links, it felt it could organise the attempt with minimum direct costs, although considerable staff time would be required.

The two issues to be addressed were the underwriting of the project costs and the nature and payment of any necessary promotional activity. The charity hoped the company would see the benefits of the idea and could be persuaded to fund the point-of-sale material and offer a minimum guarantee of income to the charity.

Sadly, this was not the case. Although keen to proceed with the idea, the company felt that promotional costs should be paid out of the proceeds of the badge sales. This naturally caused Charity Y some concerns: although it felt the plan was financially viable, the level of income would be dependent upon the level of support given by the company and its staff, particularly through the selling of the badges. Without a minimum guarantee of income, the charity could be in the position of putting in a great deal of valuable time while facing a risk that the expected income might not materialise. Of equal importance was the issue of payment of promotional costs: if these were to be paid from the proceeds of badge sales, would this be misleading the public, who would otherwise imagine that they were contributing directly to the charity?

Considering all the issues, Charity Y concluded that it was not only ethically wrong, but publicly unacceptable, for the costs of promotional materials to be paid from money given (if not technically donated) by the public. Furthermore, and without a minimum guarantee from the company to indicate its support for the project, the risk of the partnership not achieving an appropriate level of net income for the charity was too high. The charity therefore contacted the company and announced that it was turning down its offer of being the Charity of the Year.

# Case study 2 – the Royal Society for the Protection of Birds: an environmental policy for business partnerships *Adrian Penrose*

## Background

As Europe's largest wildlife conservation organisation, the Royal Society for the Protection of Birds (RSPB) has an environmental policy to guide its fundraising partnerships with the corporate sector. This policy is evolving to embrace all the RSPB's relationships with commercial organisations.

In the late 1980s, the RSPB returned a donation from an international oil company as a result of a conflict of interests when an officially designated wildlife site was damaged by the company.

Since then, the RSPB has taken a holistic approach to relationships with commercial organisations. Its identity and reputation are among the most valuable assets that the Society possesses. The RSPB's relationship with the corporate sector can be at the forefront of RSPB identity recognition, and provide broad exposure to many individuals, from consumers to decision makers. The application of a consistent approach to the business sector in its conservation, marketing and communications work is, therefore, essential if these relationships are to be a force for good. In time, the RSPB will create a policy that includes suppliers, companies in which it invests, companies that approach the Society for help or advice, and companies approached by the RSPB with a view to forming a relationship for any benefit, financial or otherwise.

In general terms, the RSPB seeks to meet four aims. First, relationships should raise positively the profile of the Society and its work. Second, corporate relationships should add value to the membership experience in some way. Third, relationships should provide significant and sustainable revenue. Fourth, the RSPB is keen to establish relationships that are commensurate with its goals and objectives and that benefit conservation either through the direct action of the company, the revenue generated, or through the mobilisation of consumers, employees or suppliers.

There are several reasons for adopting an environmental policy:

- Potential business partners need to be aware of the environmental standards expected of them before they enter a relationship with the RSPB.

- A clear policy ensures consistency of decision making internally and prevents the personal views of staff influencing what should be corporate decisions.

- As an organisation with over one million members, whose financial and other support is fundamental to its success, a clear framework for communication and for protecting the RSPB's reputation is essential.

- A clear policy provides more appropriate targeting and management of potential business partners.

# Devising the policy

In devising the policy, the starting point for the RSPB was the principle that it wishes to be a positive force for good within boardrooms across the UK, welcomed into constructive dialogue with a view to forming mutually beneficial partnerships that directly or indirectly benefit wild birds, other wildlife and their habitats. A number of questions were posed during the early planning stages of the policy.

First, what right did the RSPB have to question the activity of other companies? It became clear that the RSPB would need to ensure its own house was in order before placing expectations on corporate partners: this led to an internal 'green audit' and an extensive programme of internal environmental performance improvement. For an environmental organisation, this was, of course, a desirable step in itself.

Second, should the RSPB set up an operation to conduct environmental audits for companies? Although it was felt that companies might expect this of the organisation, the Society came to the conclusion that, as this service is widely available in the market place, offering it would be an inappropriate use of charitable funds.

Third, how could the views and wishes of the membership be incorporated into any policy? The simple solution to this was to use omnibus surveys to question members at regular intervals about their views on business and ethical issues and to respond accordingly.

Fourth, what internal processes would be needed for the efficient and objective implementation of the policy? The processes devised are outlined below, but are evolving to take account of new best practices.

In the early 1990s, the RSPB liaised with two organisations that were already viewed with credibility by the corporate sector. These were the CBI's Environment Business Forum and the International Chambers of Commerce Business Charter for Sustainable Development. It was agreed that the environmental requirements and principles of these two organisations would become the basis of the RSPB's policy.

It was also considered important to include four commitments to conservation that companies would be expected to support. Finally, as far as the members' views were concerned, the policy made clear that any link with a business partner should be compatible with the values of its membership.

In order to ensure that companies were clear about the implications of agreeing to abide by the RSPB's policy, the final element of the policy covered the RSPB's right to dissociate itself from any business relationship should it feel that the policy was being contravened in any way.

## Implementation of the policy

There were three initial stages in the implementation of the policy:

- Fundraisers would use the policy to help select companies that they felt would be likely to endorse the policy. By doing so, they would avoid wasting time approaching companies where there was a high risk that the partnership could not develop.

- Whether the company had approached the RSPB, or whether a fundraiser was planning an approach, a request would be made to the co-ordinating member of staff for permission to enter into discussions with the company.

- The co-ordinator would circulate the request the to a pre-selected group of RSPB staff, representing a range of interests and experiences in the organisation (in support of the environmental policy, all requests and replies are made by e-mail). The group would be asked to reply within three days, as a reflection of the urgency with which potential corporate partnership needs to be considered. A decision would be based on the outcome of the responses and of a 'self-help' questionnaire that would be completed by the staff fundraiser. Staff also use the additional resources of the Electronic Telegraph archives and the Ethical Investment Research Service (EIRIS). A select group of six people act as an 'arbitration service', should the response from the initial research be inconclusive.

## RSPB Working with Business Policy

The RSPB's initial policy embraced two recognised guidelines for the environmentally acceptable conduct of business:

- the requirements for membership of the CBI's Environment Business Forum;
- the principles laid down in the International Chambers of Commerce Business Charter for Sustainable Development.

More recently, as environmental reporting has started to improve and expectations have changed, this policy has been refined to create a framework of standards comprising a number of criteria commonly requested by other 'standard setters'. In addition, there are some criteria specific to the RSPB and recognition of the Nine Principles of the UN Global Compact. There are no current legislative requirements for the disclosure of non-financial environmental information. The range of company reporting styles is wide, and there are many areas requiring subjective decisions. Nevertheless, the RSPB asks that business partners abide by these in practice, or demonstrate an agreed longer-term intention to achieve these principles in practice.

Some points of emphasis in the revised draft RSPB Working with Business Policy include the commitment:

- to avoid developments involving land notified as a Site of Special Scientific Interest (SSSI), an Area of Special Scientific Interest (ASSI – in Northern Ireland), a Special Protection Area (SPA), a 'Ramsar' site, or candidates for such designations, as well as protected land outside the UK;
- potentially, in the construction of projects where there is no statutory process to protect wildlife, to plan proactively to avoid damaging developments;
- to actively avoid any adverse impact on bird species specified on the 'red' or 'amber' listings in the UK Biodiversity Action Plan;
- that all UK and EU legislation designed to protect wildlife is upheld;
- that there is no involvement in directly passing technology agreed as environmentally unsound to developing countries.

In addition, the RSPB requires potential commercial partners, as a minimum, to have or be working towards:

- a corporate environmental policy;
- the designation of a director with environmental responsibilities;
- setting targets and processes for enacting an environmental policy;
- publication of a verified annual environmental report.

RSPB business partnerships are initiated with the best intent and on the basis of mutual understanding. However, situations may arise in which a link with a current or prospective business partner could be seen as incompatible with the RSPB's conservation mission and its membership. In such instances, every effort will be made to achieve a mutually acceptable solution, but the RSPB always retains the right to dissociate from a business relationship and comment on the circumstances as necessary. The RSPB's policies in this field will continue to evolve.

# Case study 3 – an ethical conundrum

## Background

This case study concerns a development agency, whose principal mission was to remove from places of war and danger refugees (particularly children and women) who, through no fault of their own, were placed at risk by the fighting. The case in question occurred in the countries of former Yugoslavia, at a time when some of the most ferocious and horrendous incidents were taking place, and when 'ethnic cleansing' was being carried out by some of the warring factions.

Like many other development agencies, this particular agency had a well-established ethical policy in respect of receipt of support from commercial organisations. After broad and public consultation with its supporter base, the organisation had established the principle that it would not seek, or receive, support from commercial organisations that were involved in the armaments industry. The justification for this position was that the objects of any armaments company were antithetical to the core object and mission of the agency.

## A problem requiring an immediate response

As part of its work in former Yugoslavia, the agency was at the forefront of efforts to remove from areas of enormous danger and terror those refugees who, by virtue of their ethnic minority status, were being subjected to intimidation and physical abuse. One particular group of refugees, trapped in one of the more remote enclaves, had deservedly achieved considerable media attention, and there was great concern for their future well-being, indeed for their very survival. The charity was making great efforts (covered on the television screens of countries throughout the world) to remove these refugees to a place of safety. However, the geographical remoteness of the enclave and the nature of the terrain between the refugees' point of siege and the sanctuary of the UN lines meant that the efforts of the agency had thus far been unsuccessful. The only vehicles able to effect the safe transport of the refugees from the enclave to the sanctuary were a particular type of armoured carrier, which the charity had neither access to nor the resources to purchase. It was quite clear that this desperate situation would be resolved, positively or negatively, within the following 48 hours.

## A knight in tarnished armour

At this time of considerable stress and turmoil, when the actions of the charity itself were under intense media scrutiny, a commercial organisation offered to provide a fleet of six such armoured carriers within a 24-hour period to enable all the refugees to be transported safely and securely outside the enclave.

Acceptance of this donation, which the company offered with only one stipulation, would have enabled the charity to achieve its charitable objects and mission and remove all the refugees from their place of danger. Failure to act, and to act quickly, would almost certainly lead to the death of the refugees.

However, the charity's director of fundraising was faced with a particular ethical dilemma that was a result of the nature of the company concerned and the stipulation that the company was attaching to the gift of the armoured carriers.

The company concerned was an armaments company. Not only was it an armaments company, but the very equipment being used by the warring factions in former Yugoslavia was certain to have come – in part at least – from the company itself. Further, in offering to donate the armoured carriers, the company had stipulated that each of the fleet of armoured carriers must have the full company name and company logo emblazoned on all sides of the truck. This stipulation was clearly made in the knowledge that media coverage of the refugees' evacuation would achieve prime-time television coverage throughout the world.

## Resolving the dilemma

So, what was the director of fundraising to do? On the one hand, the charity could accept the gift and thereby – possibly only thereby – ensure the evacuation of the refugees and the achievement of the charity's mission; but the charity could only do this by disregarding its ethical policy, formulated with the full agreement of the charity's existing members (who were supporting the work of the agency in the enclave), not to accept support from armaments companies. On the other hand, the charity could refuse the offer of support, thereby complying with the ethical code of practice agreed with its supporter base; but in so doing it would expose to continuing danger and possible death the refugees whom the charity existed to help.

The director of fundraising contacted the Institute of Fundraising and asked for advice and guidance on the practical course of action that he should take. The Institute of Fundraising's advice was that the charity had no option but to accept the support, since the organisation would otherwise not be able to address its core mission. The charity wrote to all its existing supporters explaining the dilemma it faced and indicating why it had taken the action it had. Although this was not intended as a fundraising appeal, the letter raised more money than any other previous appeal.

# Case histories
– the company
perspective

# CHAPTER FOURTEEN

# Whitbread – resource transfer in action

**Brenda Roberts**

# Introduction

The transition from paternalistic company philanthropy to corporate community involvement (CCI), in which specific benefits to both sectors are identified, has brought radical changes to the relationship between organisations (both public and private) and the communities in which they operate and of which they are a part. Up until the 1980s the accepted means of supporting the community was to provide charitable donations for non-specific purposes. As far as Whitbread and a number of other businesses were concerned, 1981 changed that approach: events such as the Brixton riots provided a graphic and frightening example of what society might be like if government were left to cope with those problems on its own. It was no accident that Business in the Community (BitC) was founded in that year, and, in a parallel initiative, Whitbread set up a dedicated community team with direct responsibility to its main board.

The next ten years proved a time for learning: businesses struggled to understand their respective role in the community, and community organisations (overcoming initial suspicions) learnt how to harness this new resource for community benefit. Partnerships blossomed with schools, small businesses and voluntary organisations, particularly those involved with issues such as youth exclusion and crime prevention. These partnerships were largely of a financial kind, although some personnel assistance was given.

A year of sharp change in CCI followed in 1991, as certain organisations recognised a huge additional resource that could be made available to the community – their employees.

# Encouraging employee volunteering

Many employees had of course already been volunteering as individuals, but what was missing was the support and encouragement of, and recognition from, their employers. To change this, a model was followed that originated in the US, where most corporations recognised the value that their employees could bring to local communities. Volunteering was, and still is today, more ingrained in US culture, stretching back to the pioneering days when giving voluntary assistance was vital, standard practice and often life-saving.

In May 1991, BitC, the Volunteer Centre UK (now the National Centre for Volunteering) and Whitbread launched the Employees in the Community Initiative. Eight companies joined the leadership team, and a guide to employee volunteering was published. The initial scale of these developments was exemplified by the number of entrants to the Whitbread-sponsored award for companies that encouraged their employees to volunteer. In the first year there were a mere five entries, but a swift acceleration followed, and the 2000 award generated over 1,000 entries.

Whitbread's initial support for employee volunteers concentrated on its larger sites, where 100 or more staff were working. Having communicated the purpose of the initiative to local management, staff were then encouraged to set up small committees to examine how they could assist their local communities. Some projects emanated from the staff, some in response to requests from local organisations, and some through links with the local volunteer bureau. Committees were encouraged to become involved in hands-on activity, in addition to fundraising, and this was generally considered more satisfying by those involved. Whitbread supplied a dedicated manager, charitable funds to be used locally at the discretion of the volunteers, some company time and facilities, and, crucially, it provided various forms of recognition, including an annual event hosted by the chairman and the board. Thirty-three committees now operate in Whitbread Group across the UK, each with a small, dedicated team, but with the ability to mobilise much larger numbers, depending on the size of projects undertaken. Here are two examples of such activity:

- Travel Inn and Brewsters staff at Moor Farm Cramlington in Northumberland organise days out to the Fun Factory for groups of children from East Hartford Special Needs School. Four or five times a year children aged 4 to 10 come to play games and have lunch.

- Marriott staff at Bristol City Centre take part in the Avon Gorge Abseil on behalf of Macmillan Cancer Relief. They also arrange an annual Easter party for the pupils of Kingsweston School, where some of the children have severe learning difficulties.

The Whitbread business includes many sites with too few members of staff to form committees – for example Pizza Hut or Costa – but volunteers in these outlets are encouraged and recognised by the Whitbread Award for Volunteer Effort (WAVE). As long as individuals show a commitment to volunteering by fundraising or giving up time, then they are eligible for an annual award of up to £200 for the organisation they are supporting. These awards are available to employees and pensioners.

## Additional benefits to company and staff

Encouraging employee volunteers has had another, unexpected bonus: staff development, both for individuals and for groups. Management observed positive changes in areas such as confidence, team work, communications and presentation skills. Pilot programmes were set up to test whether structured training using community projects could replicate these benefits.

Team building in Whitbread had traditionally been tackled by sending groups to remote areas for a weekend to build temporary bridges over streams and perform other non-productive tasks. The process worked, but now groups embark on real community tasks that achieve the same team-building end but involve the completion of a worthwhile project: this activity provides much more personal satisfaction and raises the image of Whitbread in the local community. A recent challenge in Luton involved the Whitbread Group Procurement team, which took part in a 'Ground Force' project to transform derelict land at the local Luton & Dunstable Hospital into a beautiful garden retreat. The team challenge has now become an annual event for this team and many others in Whitbread.

Individual development is being tackled by community development assignments. Having identified a personal development need, a not-for-profit organisation, such as BitC, is asked to identify a community project that will meet the individual requirement but also benefit the community. It is planned, executed and evaluated exactly as any other training discipline, but it additionally provides community benefit. For example, one of the maintenance team at Newcastle Marriott improved his communication and organisation skills by managing an environmental project for Throckley Pond Nature Reserve.

Building on the outcomes from our volunteering experiences, we expect that community involvement projects will become part of the menu of development opportunities available to Whitbread employees. The resource of company employees, whether as volunteers or as individuals directed to become involved with the community for developmental purposes, is growing and has already become a potent force in community activity.

# Unlocking other company resources

The majority of the leading companies in CCI are now involved in contributing money and people resources. The next objective is to release the myriad other resources that companies can offer. There is, first, the huge bank of skills and experience that companies like Whitbread possess and are prepared to offer to the voluntary sector on an occasional basis. By this process, schools, colleges and universities gain from the business skills available from Whitbread school governors or board members, and volunteering organisations benefit from trustee involvement and more general advice. Examples have included: the redesign of the kitchen and catering area for a foyer in Scotland by a Beefeater manager; the use of Whitbread's procurement team to advise on the process of tendering; and Whitbread's logistics expertise, which ensured that the 30,000 meals required by the disabled athletes at the Special Olympics were available at the right times and in the right place. The inevitable widening of the network of contacts through a business involvement should not be underestimated. In some cases, our contacts have provided very large financial savings to organisations in the voluntary sector.

Space in and around buildings will sometimes become surplus to an organisation's needs. This may be short term – as in the case of Costa Coffee, where a two-year end-of-lease situation enabled a homeless centre to offer training space in central London. Or it may be longer term – as in Salford, where three floors above a pub were converted into 27 small workshops for start-up businesses. Restaurant car parks can also be made available for mobile libraries, and offices in city centres 'loaned' to voluntary agencies for meetings.

## Reassigning resources

By far the biggest opportunity in the 'other' resources area is for companies to identify all those items that they no longer need and which, despite being in good condition, would normally be consigned to the scrap heap. Until 1997, Whitbread adopted a policy of trying to supply individual items requested from time to time by community organisations: a table and chairs, a computer, some carpeting – in other words, by reacting to community needs. Then we decided to trial a proactive approach, which we began by piloting a community resources project in the Hotels division.

Marriott Hotels and Travel Inns account for over 330 hotels and almost 24,000 rooms in the UK and, importantly for this project, have a rolling refurbishment programme. From the hotels' point of view, a critical factor in refurbishment is how quickly the individual rooms can be brought back into service. Previously, unwanted items of furniture were disposed of by the contractor. Not any more. Now the details of refurbishments are forwarded as they are being planned to the community investment programme, which then plans their 'second life'. Beds, carpets, wardrobes, curtains, sofas, chairs and mirrors are entered on the resources database and matched with the needs of community organisations held on file. The organisations are then invited to collect the goods as soon as the refurbishment commences. When the Swallow International in London's Knightsbridge was due to be upgraded and rebranded as a Marriott, Whitbread's community team reviewed its database for charities within the hotel's postcode district and found that YMCA England had previously expressed an interest in furniture. A telephone call confirmed that nine of the organisation's YMCAs were very much in the market, and arrangements were made for the contents of 90 bedrooms to be collected, as well as reception and banqueting furniture.

Activities such as this have encouraged Whitbread to develop the concept across the whole of its business, and a full time co-ordinator has been appointed to manage the operation. The community opportunity in a company such as Whitbread is enormous. It can examine items no longer required in restaurants, leisure centres, hotels and offices. The potential for community benefit that could be achieved if all businesses adopted a proactive stance to surplus requirements is immeasurable.

# Beyond financial donations

The provision of financial donations to the community by business will always be important, but will always be of a limited nature. Donations of gifts in time and gifts in kind can add so much to the fabric of the community and can play to the strengths of commercial organisations by using all their resources.

## Review imminent

Whitbread is currently conducting a review of its CCI programme. The aim is to carry on making a significant impact in its chosen area of support under the new umbrella theme of 'helping young people achieve their potential'. At the same time, the company aims to achieve specific and measurable benefits for the new Whitbread business.

# CHAPTER FIFTEEN

# One 2 One*: making a positive difference

**Toby Hester**

## Football, the FA Charity Shield, and the mobile phone industry

The success of One 2 One's inaugural sponsorship of the FA Charity Shield in August 1999 marked the beginning of a continuing programme of sponsorship opportunities to increase the company's profile and involvement in the football community. As the flagship of charitable activity in football, the FA Charity Shield has raised millions of pounds for many charities over the years and was seen as the perfect platform for the company to launch its new social and community programme.

The mobile-phone industry is one of the most highly competitive market places in the UK. At the time of going to press, more than 24 million people own a mobile phone in the UK, and this figure is expected to double to approximately 46 million in the following two years. Against this background, the major players in the industry are locked in fierce competition to become market leaders, with market share and brand loyalty the ultimate and highly coveted symbols of success.

For both One 2 One and its competitors, sponsorship is a major communications tool that is used to help reach and positively influence a broad, often diverse, audience. Sponsorship enables companies to build relationships with target groups as well as increase awareness of their brand and their associated values.

Football is the nation's sport and is watched and enjoyed by millions. It brings together a hugely diverse group of people – men, women, and families; old and young; rich and poor – in ways that no other sport can. Football is also a game of passion: people who

---

*One 2 One became T-Mobile in April 2002: this case study predates that name change.

watch and play football do so passionately, and issues connected with football elicit often passionate comment and debate in all walks of society.

For One 2 One, sports sponsorship – particularly in the football market – has formed an important tool for increasing awareness of the One 2 One brand and the caring, enabling and passionate values it stands for. Football's wide appeal presents a fantastic means of reaching One 2 One's own broad target market; it is also seen as a perfect reflection of One 2 One's aim to connect its customers with the things they care passionately about – such as families, friends and football. Football allows One 2 One to demonstrate how it can seamlessly and effortlessly bring people together, both in terms of technical communications, and in ways that are mutually beneficial to the company and the customers it serves.

# Laying the foundations for social marketing

Over recent years, One 2 One has developed a vigorous brand-led social marketing programme to support market share growth and increase brand loyalty. It has achieved this through the strategic use of football sponsorship, in particular the acquisition of a number of key football-sponsorship assets, among which the following have been acquired since 1996:

- the FA Charity Shield
- Football Associate status – the official mobile-phone provider for the England team
- sponsorship of Everton FC
- sponsorship of Rotherham United FC.

The combined effect of these sponsorship programmes (each of which has to meet individual objectives) is to give One 2 One a conspicuously strong presence in the football market, which enables it to achieve its corporate and commercial objectives of increasing market share and strengthening customer loyalty.

These objectives may be summarised as:

- becoming the champion of football's charitable causes
- becoming a credible part of the football experience
- maximising awareness of the One 2 One brand and services among football actives.

## Standing out from the crowd

However, the football-sponsorship market is increasingly crowded, and both One 2 One's profile as a football sponsor and also its sponsorship budgets were relatively low in comparison with the sport's other sponsors such as Nike, Axa, and Carling. Market positioning and clear differentiation were key to ensuring One 2 One achieved its objectives and gained maximum return on its investments.

In June 1999, Cause & Effect Marketing, the strategic values-marketing consultancy, conducted a detailed programme of research into English football to identify a social context that would allow One 2 One to connect its objectives with the football community. As part of the research, Cause & Effect Marketing looked at football's governing bodies and the initiatives put in place by other sponsors, competitors and commercial and not-for-profit organisations. Of particular interest were the relationships these initiatives had established with football, football fans and their wider communities.

First, Cause & Effect Marketing identified that, for One 2 One to be accepted as the 'champion of football's charity causes' (the company's primary objective), its programme of social marketing activities needed to have conspicuous genuineness and integrity – true demonstrations of the company's over-arching brand-sponsorship philosophy 'to make a positive difference to fans' lives'.

Second, for One 2 One to be recognised as a 'credible part of the football experience', Cause & Effect Marketing recommended that One 2 One actively sought (and engaged in) regular dialogue with football supporters in order to understand the issues that most resonated with them. Results of joint research subsequently conducted by One 2 One and the Football Supporters' Association (FSA) helped validate the cause-related marketing strategy adopted by One 2 One:

- 95 per cent of fans said they were looking to companies to do more than commercially exploit the national game;
- over 60 per cent of fans added that they would like to see increased football development for disabled players.

As a result, One 2 One's cause-related marketing strategy focused on earning One 2 One a credible position in the football world by positioning One 2 One as the champion of football's disability causes.

Using its primary football sponsorship, the One 2 One FA Charity Shield, as the flagship for developing a cause-related marketing programme, the strategy was therefore to create a niche market focus on disability football that would not only deliver tangible end-user benefits (i.e. increased football opportunities for disabled people), but would also demonstrate that One 2 One was a brand with a soul, able to 'make a positive difference to fans' lives'.

As a result, One 2 One implemented a programme of disability issue sponsorships centring on:

- One 2 One Ability Counts – a programme that provides quality football opportunities for disabled people, in partnership with the English Federation of Disability Sport (EFDS) and the Football Association;

- the National Association of Disabled Supporters (NADS), an independent body which the government has commissioned to audit facilities for disabled football fans at all 114 premier and league clubs in England and Wales.

# Sponsorship and cause-related marketing strategies

*'Making a positive difference to people's lives' is at the heart of One 2 One's brand and sponsorship objectives and upholds One 2 One's positioning 'Supporting football for disabled people'.*

By providing equal opportunities for disabled people to watch and also to play the nation's game, One 2 One is able to demonstrate its human and caring brand values and also to show that, through carefully targeted sponsorship, it can help to make a tangible, positive difference to people's lives through football.

**FIGURE 6** THE ONE 2 ONE ABILITY COUNTS PROGRAMME

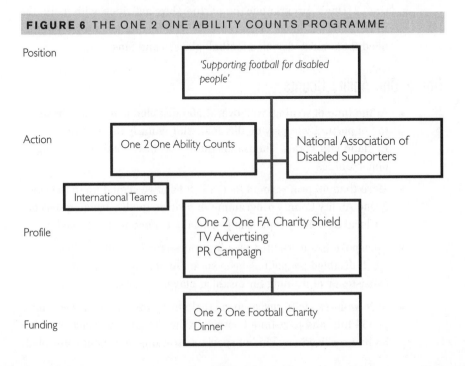

The One 2 One Ability Counts programme (Figure 6) is a first-class example of how One 2 One, in partnership with the EFDS and the FA, is working to change the face of disabled football. By taking an approach to sponsoring disability football in England that includes both supporter and player (via NADS and the EFDS), One 2 One is able to demonstrate its long-term commitment to making a tangible and positive difference to people's lives through football, and thereby to reflect the company's brand values of connecting and enabling people.

Importantly for One 2 One, the company's involvement in the Ability Counts programme is not simply about donating funds. By leveraging its connections in the football world through all its sponsorship assets, One 2 One is able to show that disability does not mean inability. The company has encouraged its other football and commercial partners not only to support the Ability Counts programme, but also to make a commitment to raising the profile of disability football and funds to channel into it. In this way, the One 2 One Ability Counts programme benefits over the longer term, as funds are generated on a continuing basis from a wide range of sources, which is of greater benefit than one-off quick injections of cash.

# Delivering tangible results

One 2 One's programme of partnership activities with both the EFDS and NADS has delivered clear-cut results for the people that need them most: disabled football players and fans.

## One 2 One Ability Counts

- At the time of writing, well over 2,500 disabled people now have the opportunity to play quality football regularly throughout England and Wales. Thousands more now have football coaching opportunities.

- More than 40 professional football clubs have signed up to the One 2 One Ability Counts programme to provide quality training sessions for local disabled people using specially trained football coaches.

- A bespoke FA-accredited training course for football coaches to teach disabled people has been set up to ensure quality and consistency of training for disabled players across the country.

- In November 1999, research carried out by the EFDS showed that of 554 full- and part-time Football in the Community coaches, only 38 had received any kind of specialist training in coaching disabled people. In the first six months following the launch of One 2 One Ability Counts, more than 170 coaches from professional football clubs and local authorities had successfully completed the 'Coaching Disabled Footballers' course. This number continues to rise and, two years on, stands at around 490.

- Five regional squads have been created for players with a learning disability. Squads for other disabilities are being built.

- A competitive structure has been set up to give the best disabled players a chance to progress from local to national level.

- A number of high-profile football celebrities have been used to highlight the programme, including Kevin Keegan and Denis Wise, helping to gain widespread media coverage and draw attention to the issues surrounding disability football in a positive way. In addition, key football opinion formers have been encouraged to sign their clubs/organisations up to the programme and commit to its standards.

- Comprehensive national and local media, advertising and brand awareness campaigns have been implemented each year for the One 2 One Charity Shield, underpinning One 2 One's long-term commitment to disability football. There is also continuing PR and media support for the programme at all levels – from local disabled football festivals to in-depth coverage focusing on the England National Disabled Squads at international tournaments around the world.

- One 2 One Ability Counts was the focus of the 2000 One 2 One Charity Shield gala fundraising dinner, the company's flagship event. Keegan lobbied his peers to raise £85,000 for the EFDS.

- A high-impact awareness video, *See the Ability – not the Disability*, has been produced to highlight the importance of the programme to football bodies and clubs, local authorities, schools, etc.

- A One 2 One Ability Counts web site has been created to enable disabled people across the country to have ready access to information about disability football and local playing opportunities.

### NADS

- A nationwide audit of all 114 English football club stadia and their disabled facilities has been conducted at the request of the government. The results have been published in NADS's *Guide to Grounds*, which is available to all clubs and their disabled supporters. Lobbying for improved facilities continues at the highest levels.

- NADS's web site (www.NADS.org.uk) has been developed to provide regular two-way communication with disabled fans.

# Benefits all round
## For One 2 One ...

Measured against the company's core sponsorship objectives set out at the beginning of the programme, One 2 One's disability sponsorship programme has achieved some significant results.

- One 2 One has become the champion of football's charitable causes:
    - In just two years, the company's brand-tracking research shows that 14 per cent of One 2 One's 8.2 million customers acknowledge the company's charitable support of football as a result of their sponsorship of the FA Charity Shield
    - 38 per cent of football fans recognise the need for football opportunities for disabled people.
- One 2 One has become a credible part of the football experience:
    - 27 per cent of football fans recognise One 2 One's support for disabled people in football, according to a survey conducted for One 2 One.
    - In November 2000, the One 2 One Ability Counts programme won the overall best Sportsmatch sponsorship of grassroots sport. It was also category winner for disabled sport.
- The sponsorship programme has maximised awareness of the One 2 One brand and services among people active in football:
    - 44 per cent of football fans recognise One 2 One as a sponsor in football.

Such high-level public recognition of the success of the One 2 One Ability Counts programme – particularly given the relatively short period of time since the programme's inception – is proof of the real benefits experienced by disabled football fans and is testament to the close partnership among the programme's backers.

## For the EFDS ...

The EFDS is the official, national umbrella body responsible for the co-ordination and development of sport for disabled people in England. It believes that sport is for everyone and that disabled people have a right to a wide range of sporting choices and opportunities as a matter of common practice. Its objectives are threefold:

- to be the united voice of disability sport in England;

- to influence organisational policies, practices and structures to promote mainstreaming of disability sport from grassroots through to excellence;

- to campaign for increased and improved sporting choices and opportunities for disabled people.

One 2 One's sponsorship of the Ability Counts programme has secured significant funds for the EFDS. Working with the support of One 2 One and the Football Association, and alongside other backers of the One 2 One Ability Counts programme (Umbro and Sportsmatch), the EFDS has been able to raise awareness at the highest levels of the need for equal rights for disabled people to play and enjoy the game. For example, under the umbrella of the One 2 One FA Charity Shield, demonstration matches of disability football have been played to capacity audiences at both Wembley and the new Millennium Stadium, and more than 50 premier and league clubs in England have signed up to provide regular, quality playing opportunities for disabled people. It is estimated that under the One 2 One Ability Counts programme, more than 1,500 disabled people, many of them young people, now have the opportunity to play quality football regularly. This number is expected to continue to rise as the number of clubs involved increases. The additional publicity generated by One 2 One – terrestrial and Sky TV campaigns, national press, PR and advertising and pitch-side displays – also significantly increases the profile of disability football and the need for equal opportunities.

# For NADS ...

As a newly convened charity, the National Association of Disabled Supporters (NADS) has benefited from the increased awareness and public recognition of its work provided by One 2 One's financial backing and professional guidance. For example, One 2 One provided celebrity footballers to promote the work of NADS, which helped to gain widespread national coverage for both organisations in key national and regional publicity campaigns, thus raising awareness of the work of the charity and the issues it was seeking to address.

Furthermore, both government and One 2 One's corporate backing of NADS has opened doors to other professional football organisations such as the Football Association, the Professional Footballer's Association and the Football Foundation – thereby ensuring a continued high profile for its work and charitable aims.

And finally, One 2 One's financial backing has allowed NADS's committee members to flourish and to become more able to meet the needs of its members via improved access to telecommunications and web technology.

# Conclusions and lessons learnt

As this case study demonstrates, One 2 One's disability sports sponsorship programme has achieved some tremendous successes since its inception in 1999. The fact that end users – disabled people – can so readily see and reap the tangible benefits of the programme is testament to this success. All parties' determination and will to achieve the ultimate aims of the programme also need to be recognised as significant factors in the programme's overall success.

However, aligning the broad-based, challenging corporate objectives of a major blue chip company with the tighter, more focused objectives of smaller charities has its challenges. Cultural and commercial differences, combined with inevitable tightening of both human and financial resources, can at times make the best of partnerships feel under strain.

Ever-changing business priorities, and commercial pressure to gain the competitive edge, make the fast-moving world of telecommunications a volatile place to operate. Under increasing pressure to show market cut-through as value for sponsorship, One 2 One has to place considerable pressure on all its partners to deliver the end results it seeks. Both NADS and the EFDS therefore have to show how they contribute to the achievement of One 2 One's overall sponsorship objectives. There are many criteria for measuring success – such as increased corporate profile and public recognition for their charitable activities – but none are so strong as increased sales or improved customer loyalty. Proving how they have contributed to these core criteria will be crucial to the long-term viability of the partnerships.

As with any successful partnership, effective relationship management is essential to success: this is not always straightforward.

# CHAPTER SIXTEEN

# From CCI towards an integrated social policy and ... a better world

**Adrian Hosford**

## A decade's corporate community programme, and how to develop it

For more than a decade now BT has operated one of the UK's most extensive corporate community programmes and, cast into a leadership position, has been concerned to lead well.

The company's community and social activities have always aimed not only to reflect its commitment to good citizenship, but also directly to assist BT's public standing and reputation, which we regard as one of the company's strategic commercial assets. The company is conscious that people do not just 'buy' products; they also 'buy' the organisation behind the product. Our approach is not therefore just philanthropy, but a measured investment that can, and should, be justified to all the company's stakeholders.

As a founder member of the Per Cent Club, BT has consistently set aside at least half a per cent of its pre-tax profits for community causes (as defined by Business in the Community – BitC) and is now a full one per cent member.

In the early 1990s, however, BT effectively divided its support between six separate areas. Although this enabled us to assist a broad range of activities, the programme was arguably more philanthropic than it was effective – not exactly our intention!

A large portfolio of over 150 projects meant that the programme's impact was diffuse, and that, despite its size, it seemed overall to be garnering only modest recognition. This somewhat reactive stance obviously made it somewhat difficult to demonstrate any real connection with BT's mainstream activities.

These issues were, however, tackled in a strategic review in the mid-1990s, which led to an updated mission statement for the community programme, new objectives and fresh project selection criteria.

## A new mission statement, and its effect

The change to the mission was striking. Previously, the programme's main direction had been drawn simply from one of BT's overall corporate aims 'to make a fitting contribution to the community in which it conducts its business'. A far more focused role was now defined for the community programme, maintaining the old goals but additionally emphasising relevance to the company. The new mission statement read:

*BT is committed to a programme of investment in and partnership with external organisations which: demonstrably improves the quality of life and well-being of the communities in which BT operates around the world; builds and maintains the company's reputation; provides a source of pride in the company for its employees and a means for their involvement and participation in the community; and enhances BT's business.*

BT also wanted to improve its focus by adopting a unifying theme to articulate all its community activities.

In the end, we adopted the theme of 'communications skills', which provided a good fit all round, linking well with the human as well as with the physical factors of communication – a particular focus for the company. The theme also formed a natural progression from the community programme portfolio as it then stood.

The programme started to take an increasingly proactive line with charities, seeking to focus resources on specific issues related to BT's guiding themes and strengths. As a consequence, award schemes for charities were run focusing on interpersonal communications and then new technologies. These received some hundreds of applications and subsequent partnerships were based on much clearer expectations about what could be delivered. Similarly, a closer relationship was forged with the beneficiary charities of BT Swimathon, linking the projects they would undertake with the money raised by the event.

We also worked closely with the charities benefiting from 'BT Friends and Family Chosen Charities', to promote programmes relating to issues of communications skills.

In parallel with this activity, BT was also undertaking research to ensure that the programme aligned with the wishes of stakeholders. Perhaps the most significant outcome of these surveys was the identification of each group's priorities for BT. These showed clearly that the greatest area of concern was a cluster of issues to do with employability – such as education, training, and life skills – together with a strong desire for BT to help in the community on matters of health and welfare. The surveys also revealed a positive expectation that BT should support causes that are relevant to its business.

The impetus created by this change of focus and strategy certainly paid dividends, and BT received the Impact on Society Award in 1999 from BitC as 'Company of the Year', following this in 2000 with the Excellence Award for 'Investment in the Community'.

# Creating a unified approach

This success notwithstanding, many of us thought that the company may still be missing a trick. The community investment, social reputation and environmental teams operated pretty separately. BT was – and still is – facing continual organisational change, and the programme was still not well recognised and understood by the public in particular, although it still stood up very well compared with that of other companies.

Taking on board the reminder against complacency of 'Never mistake the edge of the rut for the horizon', we therefore determined, in the very moment of our awards success, to continue the evolution of our programme.

The first step was my appointment as the company's first director of social policy, with the three teams mentioned above reporting to me – another first. What next? Inevitably, we wanted to undertake some fundamental research to ensure that any subsequent programme fulfilled all our criteria for success. The programme should also bear in mind our long-term social image, which ideally should aim to be so positive that:

- governments would want us in their countries;
- local governments would want us on their patch;
- investors would want to invest in us;
- customers would feel good about buying from us;
- employees would be proud to work for us;
- potential employees would want to join us;
- partners would want to work with us.

A number of working assumptions additionally underlay our plans. The first of these was that any future social policy would need to be focused: in this area, BT could really only be famous for one thing. Second, although the policy must be aligned with the nature of BT's business, it must also be clearly seen as deserving and not in BT's self-interest. Third, it should necessarily directly involve as many stakeholders as possible and, we believed, be strongly promoted. Fourth, it should wherever possible be based on global need but exemplified through UK activities. Finally, it should be measurable and be capable of showing continuous progress.

Armed with this, we began with an analysis of the existing research available to us, which we supplemented with a further and extensive research programme among groups of stakeholders, including consumers, BT employees and opinion formers. The aim was to understand what influenced them into holding a positive perception of a company's social responsibility.

For the consumers – our customers – there was a clear wish that social spending did not involve wasting what they saw as their money, whereas employees wanted to be kept very much informed and involved and were interested in the details of how we planned to deliver our programme. Opinion formers and investors were keen to see a discerning company executing a brand-coherent social programme.

Four main drivers or levers emerged from the research, which were that the company and its policy should:

- be seen to fulfil the company's core functions in a thoughtful and caring way;
- be seen to be 'putting something back' into society by contributing to popular, needy and deserving causes;
- be seen to be part of a positive sector that is good for society and the planet;
- take a stand and campaign on a relevant theme.

None of these may appear ground-breakingly original, but the message to us was clear. If BT could use these four levers in a powerful combination *around a unifying theme*, while meeting the demands of the stakeholders, then we had an excellent chance of maximising the total effect of our CSR initiatives, both for society and also for our image as a socially responsible company.

The additional details to emerge from the research again revealed nothing dramatically new but confirmed that what we had hoped to focus on would indeed put us on the right track.

# Identifying the causes

Uppermost in the minds of all the groups were two 'needy' causes: work with children and support of charities. Children were seen as getting only one good chance in life at school, and it was considered vital that they had the best opportunities to learn. Schools were seen as chronically under-funded and under-resourced. Support for charities was clearly perceived – by consumers in particular – as the 'purest' form of giving, helping people in acute need without the direct link to a company's bottom line.

The message was that companies focusing on these two areas – in an appropriate way – would not be perceived as acting through self-interest and would be more likely to enhance their standing and reputation. Image was also likely to be affected positively if a company chose to make a stand on a relevant issue and appeared genuinely to be putting something back into society.

BT had, we felt, a good track record in working with education – and schools in particular – and we had more ideas of how we would carry this work further and make a bigger impact. Similarly, we had a fund of ideas of how to work with the voluntary sector and were particularly keen to promote these – and the partnerships we hoped to develop – more effectively than before.

There was much discussion about any potential campaign or issue on which we might take a stand, but there was only ever going to be one choice, and this would be to campaign on how communications can help society – and the planet. Tackling the issue of the 'digital divide' and social exclusion was the contribution we most wanted to make.

# Defining the content and theme of the programme

The next stage for us was to see whether we could link all that we had learnt from our research under the one unifying theme (of 'communication skills') mentioned earlier.

Again there was no lack of ideas from the team, but we nevertheless sought the help of a number of external creative agencies with experience in the field of CSR. The brief we gave them was that the theme should be 'campaignable' and should differentiate BT from other companies. Further, it should involve key target groups, with the emphasis on the public and employees, with a 'trickle-up' effect on opinion formers. Finally, it should be capable of raising the spontaneous association of BT with social responsibility.

In a way this was the most difficult task of all – which perhaps surprised us, despite the fact that we all agreed that properly encapsulating all that we were aiming to do was an absolutely crucial step in the process.

Communication is at the core of what BT does and is about. That was an obvious influence throughout the research, which also told us not to move away from the core focus we already had on communications skills and effective use of technology. This was true whether we were talking of:

- helping children to have the key communication and information and communication technologies (ICT) skills they need for the digital age;
- helping charities make more of communications in their good work;
- tackling a good cause where communication makes a real difference.

The core function of BT is to help people and organisations to communicate effectively, irrespective of distance. Doing this sensitively demands better communications skills in action. 'Better communications' is therefore the integrating factor in our strategy, but it is not quite enough. The end result of better communications is a 'better world'. So, if the unifying content of our programme is better communications, the unifying theme should be 'better world'. This idea and one other were put to members of the public and 'better world' had more appeal: the public was able to make a direct connection between how BT can contribute to this ideal and the positive aspects inherent in the phrase. (It is an ideal, of course, and, if all of this process appears in any way pretentious, then the only answer is that we will be judged on how our actions will match our words and rhetoric.)

The Better World campaign received board-level approval in BT in the middle of 2001 and we immediately began to prepare to move on it.

## Implementing the programme

BT has a long tradition of working in the voluntary sector: since the 1980s we have provided more than £25 million to charities of all sizes, touching many thousands of lives. Research with stakeholders tells us we should be supporting the most needy in society, and we have therefore decided to champion a major communications issue. This is now going forward working right across the company and involving our employees and customers too. We hope it will make a big impact on the sector.

Last October saw the launch of the BT Education Programme. This builds on the success of the BT FutureTalk in Education project, which delivered special Theatre in Education performance over two years to over 4,000 UK schools. The new programme has a tighter focus on interpersonal communications skills and is supported by a wealth of online resources to enhance the teaching of ICT (see www.bt.com/education). The teaching materials have been refined by independent feedback on the last project by the National Foundation for Educational Research (NFER) and by consultation with teachers.

BT is also in the process of finalising a Digital Divide campaign, which will involve working with four deprived communities representative of the UK population structure and helping them to make concrete improvement in the quality of life through enhanced communications. 'Digital Inclusion' web sites are also involved, and active campaigning designed to create a positive climate for change to happen.

We have been active in the months since we launched our new strategy and keen too to ensure that it develops in a way that fits the way the company is itself going forward. We had the firm support over the years of the previous chairman, Sir Iain Vallance, and our new chairman, Sir Christopher Bland, actively endorses the approach we are taking. It is perhaps therefore appropriate that Sir Christopher have the last word!

*At BT, our vision is one of individuals, organisations, communities and societies with unlimited access to one another and to a world of knowledge via communications technologies. We are committed to help people to realise their potential and achieve their goals.*

*This vision implies a social agenda – and we invite you to read all about how we meet our social responsibilities at www.bt.com/ betterworld.* (Sir Christopher Bland)

# CHAPTER SEVENTEEN

# CONCLUSION
## Valerie Morton

Despite the fact that each chapter has been written by a different author, there are a number of strands weaving through this book that highlight some of the key elements of corporate fundraising today. The four most significant of these are picked out below.

## The size of the corporate fundraising 'pot'

The assumption that companies have fixed community support budgets, and that fundraisers have to fight among themselves for their sham of this money, is too easy to make. Some of the excellent case studies in this book prove the opposite. Indeed, as outlined in Chapter 1, there is a wide range of budgets that fundraisers can gain access to, if they are able to apply a degree of creativity. This point is further demonstrated in Chapter 12, which shows how pay-roll giving can be promoted successfully to generate income for charities outside the usual corporate budgets. And the CRM examples from the NSPCC in Chapter 11 show how marketing budgets can be 'converted' successfully to charitable support.

## The need for creativity

The case study of Mencap and Transco in Chapter 9 recounts how income was generated through a link with safety. It is highly unlikely that Transco would have given such a large sum did the project not have this clear, innovative business link. The challenge to all corporate fundraisers is to continue to develop new ideas and create classic win–win partnerships.

## Adhering to best practice

Part I of this book sets out clearly the standards expected of good corporate fundraisers. It is no coincidence that without exception, the successful case studies highlighted in Part 2 have followed these guidelines. There may be divergence over which companies to target, how to approach them, the way in which the relationship is managed or the corporate fundraising team structured, but the basic principles remain the same. Bad practice inevitably results in failure. Worst of all, it adversely affects the whole of our sector

## Taking a holistic approach

Corporate social responsibility is clearly defined in Chapter 2 and is mentioned on numerous occasions throughout the book. Yet, in terms of their approach to the corporate sector, most charities continue to be compartmentalised. In the 1980s most charities with medium or large corporate fundraising teams had staff specialisation in the different disciplines of sponsorship. promotion, employee support, etc. The 1990s saw the recognition of a need for an account management approach to companies, and corporate fundraisers were expected to be able to promote the whole range of activities. Now, in the first decade of the new millennium, this needs to be taken one step further Our organisations need to recognise that companies currently use corporate social responsibility as an umbrella for issues as diverse as labour sources, disability discrimination and employment practices, and they need to reflect this when considering structures and interdepartmental systems of working.

From the perspective of a career corporate fundraiser, this is all good news. What was once, many years ago, a desk-bound job that involved sending appeal letters' to random companies is now a wide-ranging, excfting and rewarding job. As an industry, we need to get this message across to the young achievers of today, so that we may atfrad the best, most committed people to the sector.

# Appendices

# Legal and tax issues

**Stephen Lloyd**

## Introduction

This chapter covers legal and tax issues (as at autumn 2001) arising from:

- corporate fundraising and donations
- licensing by a charity of its name and/or logo
- sponsorship.

## Corporate fundraising and donations

Charities' corporate supporters will give their support in many different ways: some may be prepared to give and expect nothing in return; others may wish to get their staff involved in fundraising as a means of building 'team spirit'; others may want to give via their own charity. All these different methods of giving have potential legal consequences, which charities need to consider.

### Legal issues – donations

Charities do not normally have a legal problem in receiving donations. There may be special circumstances when they wish to refuse a donation, but they can do this only when the trustees have reasonable grounds for believing that acceptance of the donation would have an adverse impact on the charity's:

- staff
- volunteers
- supporters
- public image.

However, donations give rise to some tax issues.

### Donations and direct tax (Corporation and Income Tax)

Limited companies pay corporation tax on their profits, whereas firms (e.g. accountants) pay income tax. These are both direct taxes, as opposed to VAT, which is an indirect tax.

If a corporate donor is prepared to make a donation and expects only a minimal acknowledgement, then the gift will be eligible to be treated as a Gift Aid payment. Corporate Gift Aid works like this:

- The payment must not be subject to any condition as to repayment.

- In the case of 'close companies', the company, or any connected person, must not receive any benefit exceeding the permissible benefits. These are:

| Aggregate donations in the tax year | Aggregate value of benefits in the tax year |
| --- | --- |
| £0–£100 | 25% of the aggregate donations |
| £101–£1,000 | £25 |
| £1,001–£10,000 | 2.5% of the aggregate donations |
| £10,001 + | £250 |

A close company is one under the control of five or fewer participators. In the case of a 'non-close company' (e.g. a company quoted on the Stock Exchange), there is no limit, but Revenue practice seems to vary in treating benefits received by such a donor under Gift Aid. The best advice is to treat all corporate Gift Aid payments as subject to the overall £250 benefit limit.

- The donor must be a UK taxpayer.

### An example of Gift Aid calculation

XYZ Company makes a Gift Aid payment of £10,000 to ABC Charity.

When XYZ computes its taxable profits, the entire £10,000 will be treated as a tax-deductible payment as a charge on income. Many fundraisers think that the Gift Aid rules for companies are the same as they are for individuals and that, if a corporate donor makes a Gift Aid payment, this means that the charity can enhance the size of the gift through the tax relief. From the company's point of view, however, a donation under Gift Aid is just the same as a tax-deductible business expense: both can be offset against profits in calculating its corporation tax liability.

### Deeds of covenant

- Since 6 April 2000 all payments under Deeds of Covenant are treated as Gift Aid payments.

- Just as for individuals, a Deed of Covenant is a binding obligation on the part of the donor to give an agreed sum of money or a sum calculated in accordance with the fixed formula to a charity. Certain points must be noted:

- It is wise to use the standard form of Deed of Covenant prepared by the Inland Revenue.
- The mechanics of a payment under Deed of Covenant are identical to those under Gift Aid.
- Amend the deed only with professional advice.

### Partnerships

The examples above have been based on the donor being a company. The position is different in the case of partnerships. Partnerships are unincorporated businesses, and each partner is liable for his or her own tax bill. Consequently, when it comes to seeking donations from partnerships, a charity will have to persuade each individual partner to complete the relevant documentation in his or her name. This can be a tall order where there are over one hundred partners, as is the case with many modern firms. In some cases, the firms may have established their own charity, which will already have received payments under Gift Aid from the partners, and the firm charity will make the donation. To the disappointment of some fundraisers, this means that no further tax repayments can be obtained from the Inland Revenue, as a charity cannot itself make a payment under Gift Aid, since it is exempt from UK tax.

It must be emphasised that all these concessions on gifts to charities are subject to the condition that the donor gets no benefit in return over the permitted level. A small acknowledgement in an annual report or on a programme will not constitute a benefit; but more tangible recognition (e.g. display of the corporate supporter's logo on the annual report) will. If a charity wishes to do this it should consider making a reasonable charge to the supporter for the display of the supporter's logo; this charge will also attract VAT (see below).

### Donations and VAT

Donations and legacies are outside the scope of VAT, even if the donor receives some minor benefit (e.g. a flag), but, as the Customs and Excise pamphlet on Sponsorship (701/41/95) makes clear:

*to be treated as outside the scope of VAT, the sponsor's support must be entirely voluntary and secure nothing in return. A taxable supply will not be created by the simple acknowledgement of support such as:*

a) *giving a flag or sticker,*

b) *inclusion in a list of supporters in a programme, or on a notice,*

c) *naming a building or university chair after the donor,*

d) *putting the donor's name on the back of a seat in a theatre.*

However, as the pamphlet also makes clear, if a donor makes it a condition that his or her logo or trading name is to be displayed or that he or she is to receive some other benefit, then Customs will treat the entire payment as the consideration for a taxable supply, and the charity will have to account for tax on it.

Examples of VATable supplies include:

- naming an event after the sponsor
- display of the sponsor's name, logo or trading name
- free or reduced entry
- priority booking rights.

Many charities do display supporter's logos and are not challenged by Customs, but this cannot be regarded as a safe practice in the light of the very clear guidance quoted above. There is one major exception to this rule – where the sponsorship is part of a one-off fundraising event, the sponsorship income is treated as exempt from VAT.

### Staff fundraising

Many corporate supporters now wish to involve their staff in fundraising for the company's Charity of the Year. This support can raise a number of issues, as the following example will illustrate.

XYZ Company agrees to encourage its staff members to raise money through a sponsored swimathon for ABC Charity. The staff do this in their own time and solicit donations from the general public. The individual members of staff pay the money they have collected direct to ABC's bank account.

In this case, all that XYZ has done is to encourage staff fundraising and nothing more. Nonetheless, there will be issues that ABC Charity should be aware of in terms of controls on fundraising:

- Are the members of staff fit and proper persons to fundraise?
- Has the employer warranted that they are?
- Does the charity warn the members of staff of the controls on house-to-house collections if they are going around seeking sponsorship?
- Are the fundraisers being paid any expenses or obtaining benefits worth more than £5 per day or £500 per annum?

In terms of taxation:

- Will the charity be selling merchandise in connection with the event (e.g. T-shirts, baseball caps, etc)?

- If so, is this being done through the charity or its trading company?

- Should VAT be charged on the items sold?

In terms of risk:

- Who will be organising the event?

- Does the charity need to consider health and safety, risk and liability issues?

- If so, is there adequate insurance cover for all normal risks?

- If not, is there an agreement with the event organiser dealing with these issues?

What is the position where the corporate supporter wants to take a more proactive role, for example to advertise the fact that ABC Charity is its Charity of the Year throughout its stores? Will this be taken to mean that XYZ is thereby advertising its support? Provided the wording of the advertisements makes it clear that XYZ is facilitating fundraising and nothing else, and that XYZ is paying none of its own money to ABC, there will not be a taxation problem. However, there may be issues under the Charities Act 1992 (see below).

# Licences and charity law
## Cause-related marketing

Cause-related marketing arrangements involve charities licensing their names and/or logos to commercial partners. The name and/or logo is displayed on the commercial partner's goods or on brochures and advertisements advertising its services. The commercial partner in these circumstances is defined under the Charities Act 1992 as a 'commercial participator'. In essence, a commercial participator is someone who encourages purchases of goods or services on the grounds that some of the proceeds will go to a charitable institution or that a donation will be made.

Section 58(1) Charities Act 1992 defines a commercial participator as 'in relation to any charitable institution ... any person who: (a) carries on for gain any business other than a fundraising business, but (b) in the course of that business, engages in any promotional venture in the course of which it is represented that charitable contributions are to be given to or applied for the benefit of the institution.'

A number of the expressions used in this definition are also defined in the Act. 'Promotional venture' is defined as any 'advertising or sales campaign or any other venture undertaken for commercial purposes'. One dictionary definition of a venture is 'that which is ventured or risked in a commercial enterprise or speculation'.

'Charitable contributions' is defined as meaning:

*In relation to any representation made by any commercial participator or other person ... (a) the whole or part of (i) the consideration given for goods or services sold or supplied by him, or (ii) any proceeds (other than such consideration) of a promotional venture undertaken by him, or (b) sums given by him by way of donations in connection with the sale or supply of any such goods or services (whether the amount of such sums is determined by reference to the value of such goods or services or otherwise).*

Examples of commercial participators include: banks issuing affinity cards in partnership with charities; food companies who sell products with the charity's name and logo on the product stating '5p per packet will go to XYZ Charity'; a travel company that offers to pay 1 per cent of the price of a holiday to a named charity.

Under the Charities Act the commercial participator must have an agreement with what is called a charitable institution (normally a charity).

The agreement between the charitable institution and the commercial participator required by section 59(2) of the 1992 Act has to be in writing and signed by or on behalf of the charitable institution and the commercial participator.

The agreement has to specify:

- the name and address of each of the parties to the agreement;
- the date on which the agreement was signed by or on behalf of each of those parties;
- the period for which the agreement is to subsist;
- any terms relating to the termination of the agreement prior to the date on which that period expires;
- any terms relating to the variation of the agreement during that period.

The agreement also has to contain:

- a statement of its principal objectives and the methods to be used in pursuit of those objectives;

- provision as to the manner in which are to be determined:
  - if there is more than one charitable institution party to the agreement, the proportion in which the institutions which are so party are respectively to benefit under the agreement;
  - the proportion of the consideration given for goods or services sold or supplied by the commercial participator or of any other proceeds of a promotional venture undertaken by him or her, which is to be given to or applied for the benefit of the charitable institution; or
  - the sums by way of donations by the commercial participator in connection with the sale or supply of any goods or services sold or supplied by him or her which are to be so given or applied;

  as the case may require;

- provision as to any amount by way of remuneration or expenses which the commercial participator is to be entitled to receive in respect of things done by him in pursuance of the agreement and the manner in which any such amount is to be determined.

These requirements are the various legal minima. Charities should also consider whether or not there are other clauses that should be inserted in such a contract to cover their positions. In particular, charities should consider the fact that licensing their name to a commercial organisation can give rise to a number of problems.

## Problems of association

Each charity that enters into arrangements whereby its name is to be associated with the goods and/or services provided by a third party needs to appreciate that there is a risk that the charity's name could be brought into disrepute through the activities of the licensee or some member of its group of companies. Modern trans-national companies have tentacles spread throughout many countries. The company with which a charity has a licensing arrangement in the UK may be involved in many different industries in many parts of the world, and it is impossible for the charity to check adequately on the performance of all those companies prior to entering into any licence.

Nothing can be 100 per cent watertight in these circumstances, and charities need to proceed with considerable caution. It is therefore suggested that, where a charity is licensing its name, in addition to the requirements laid down under the Charities Act, a charity should request that the contract contain clauses such as:

- a minimum guaranteed sum payable to the charity;

- a warranty by the licensee that neither it nor any of its associated companies (i.e. subsidiaries or joint ventures) will at any time during the duration of the agreement do anything that could bring the reputation of the charity into disrepute;

- a termination clause allowing the charity to terminate the licence immediately should, in its reasonable opinion, its name be brought into disrepute by the licensee or its associates or if the licensee is in a material breach of any of the terms of the agreement;

- a term relating to what happens to stock bearing the charity's logo in the event of early termination of the agreement due to its breach by the licensee;

- strict controls on the use of the charity's name and logo and recognition of its copyright;

- mutual clearance of all publicity materials and agreed wording to describe each partner and their relationship;

- an undertaking that the commercial participator will abide at all times with all relevant health, environmental and legal obligations and codes of best practice;

- interest on late payments.

A charity might also wish to seek other clauses such as:

- an agreement that the commercial participator will not enter into a similar arrangement with any other organisation operating in the same field as the charity for the duration of the agreement;

- an indemnity in respect of any losses or damage suffered by the charity as a result of any action by the commercial participator;

- an obligation on the commercial participator to segregate moneys due to the charitable institution in a separate bank account preferably marked with the name of the charity so that, should the commercial participator go into liquidation, the moneys in the account will be deemed to be trust moneys and not part of the general assets of the commercial participator available for distribution to the general body of its creditors.

## Statements

Section 60(3) provides that, where any representation is made by a commercial participator to the effect that charitable contributions are to be given to or applied for the benefit of one or more particular charitable institutions, the representation shall be accompanied by a statement clearly indicating:

- the name or names of the institution or institutions concerned;
- if there is more than one institution concerned, the proportions in which the institutions are respectively to benefit; and
- (in general terms), the method by which it is to be determined:
  - what proportion of the consideration given for goods or services sold or supplied by him, or of any other proceeds of a promotional venture undertaken by him, is to be given to or applied for the benefit of the institution or institutions concerned; or
  - what sums by way of donations by him in connection with the sale or supply of any such goods or services are to be so given or applied,

as the case may require.

In almost all cases the statement will be made on the goods themselves or in brochures or catalogues describing the goods or services or through point-of-sale advertising.

As can be seen, there are two different ways in which the statement can be made, 'as the case may require'. Unfortunately, section 60(3) is not satisfactorily worded.

## The first possible statement

'([I]n general terms), the method by which it is to be determined (i) what proportion of the consideration given, etc' is, on close analysis, confusing. You do not need a general method to work out a proportion. Charities doing deals with commercial participators are advised to ignore completely the statement '(in general terms), the method by which it is to be determined' if possible, and seek to ensure that the statement clearly indicates what proportion of the consideration given for the goods or services sold will be given to the charitable institution concerned.

This view is substantiated by the Home Office in their publication *Charitable Fundraising: Professional and Commercial Involvement* (February 1995) where, on page 5, it is stated:

*We strongly recommend that in the case of commercial participation ... or similar activities by charitable institutions or their connected companies not subject to Part II, that the exact amount going to charitable institutions is given in the statement, expressed net (ie after deduction of all expenses, costs, etc); for example, 'X% of the purchase price goes to charity Y' or '£X per item sold goes ... etc'. Where this cannot be stated exactly then a reasonable alternative is recommended, such as 'a minimum X% ...*

*etc', or 'it is estimated that X% ... etc' provided this is a reasonable statement to make and meets the requirements of the law in the particular circumstances of the case.*

*We recommend that only where no such statement can meaningfully be made should a percentage be expressed as a gross figure. In such a case it is most important that attention is drawn in the statement to the significance of that fact, ie that further expenses will have to be paid, reducing the benefit that the charitable institution will receive from the donation.*

Seeking to deal with the problem thrown up by the phrase '(in general terms), the method by which it is to be determined, etc', the Home Office recommendations go beyond the express letter of the law in requiring rather more precise statements. Charities should be wary of agreeing to arrangements whereby they accept 'X per cent of the net profits', as this begs the question 'net of what?' If this formula is to be accepted, charitable institutions need to be very careful and thorough in agreeing what deductions can be made in order to arrive at the net profit figure: beware of such all-embracing phrases as 'management charges'. However, charities need to be realistic: it is sometimes very difficult for commercial participators to make precise statements as to what proportion of the price paid will go to the charity because of the complexities of particular commercial arrangements. Agreed minimum donations can be very useful in these circumstances.

### The second possible statement:

*(to state in general terms) the method by which it is to be determined ... what sums by way of donation by the commercial participator in connection with the sale or supply of such goods are to be given.*

The best example of this is where a charity's trading company states that '100 per cent of its taxable profits are paid to XYZ Charity'.

### Direct Tax (Corporation and Income Tax)

The surplus or profit that a charity makes from licensing its name and/or logo is not derived from carrying out the charity's purposes. A charity cannot be established to license its name and logo as a charitable activity. Licensing is a form of non-charitable trading, and any surplus is therefore liable to be taxed. The crucial points for fundraisers to bear in mind on contracts with commercial participators are as follows.

If the agreement:

- lasts for more than one year,
- and the charity only licenses its name and/or logo,
- and the charity does nothing else, e.g. co-operating on marketing or licensing its database,
- and the Inland Revenue accepts that the charity is not trading in its name and logo,

then it is possible for the payment to be made to the charity as what is called an annual payment. You should take professional advice about this; note, too, that, just because the payment is made to the charity, this does not alter the VAT position.

However, many commercial promotions last for less than a year, so that, for example, Charity A's name appears on a brand of cereal for three months. In this case, the annual payment route will not work. To avoid direct tax on any surplus on the profits from the arrangement, therefore, it is necessary to structure it so that payment is made to the charity's trading company unless the charity can show that its turnover from non-primary-purpose trading is no greater than either:

- £5,000 or
- the lesser of £50,000 and 25 per cent of the charity's gross income from all sources.

If the charity wishes to provide more services (e.g. co-operation on marketing or licensing its database), these services must always be put through the charity's trading company and an appropriate charge made.

# VAT

Customs and Excise treat the licensing by a charity, or its trading company, of its name and/or logo to a commercial partner as a taxable supply for VAT purposes. As a result, if the charity or trading company is not registered for VAT, and the price charged for the licence will bring it above the VAT registration threshold (£54,000 in 2001), it will be necessary for it to register for VAT. If it is already registered, it will have to charge VAT on the payment made by the commercial participator to the charity or its trading company. This may come as a surprise to fundraisers and the charity's corporate supporter, who will regard an on-pack promotion as advertising the corporate partner's support for the charity – but such arguments cut little ice with the VAT people. So far as they are concerned, the arrangement constitutes a payment by the commercial participator to the charity for the right to link its name with the charity's. The charity or trading company will therefore need to be told how much money is to be paid by the commercial participator and then render a VAT invoice for that amount. This can be dealt with in the agreement with the commercial participator.

In the case of affinity cards, Customs and Excise were prepared to give a concession so that 80 per cent of the payment made by the affinity card company is treated as a donation, and only 20 per cent as a payment for the right to use the charity's name and logo on the credit card and in conjunction with the advertising – which is subject to VAT. That payment is made to the charity's trading company. This unique concession applies only to affinity cards and cannot be taken as a rule of thumb for any other commercial licence.

If the commercial participator carries out VAT-exempt supplies (e.g. banking or financial services), it cannot recover any VAT charged. In such cases, the commercial participator may insist that all payments are VAT inclusive so that the charity has to account for the VAT out of the sum received. It may be possible to split the payment from the commercial participator between a charge for the use of the charity's name and logo, which will attract VAT, and a donation for the rest of the payment, which will be VAT free. Any such split must be commercially justified – in other words, the price charged for the use of the name and logo must be fair and reasonable – and, if you are considering operating such a split, you should take professional advice.

Fundraisers should also be aware that, so long as the commercial participator is registered for VAT, it is usually in the charity's interest to charge VAT, because this will increase the charity's amount of output VAT, which should in turn allow the charity to increase its rate of recovery of input VAT.

# Sponsorship

Sponsorship is a Janus word: like the Roman god, it faces two ways. Sometimes the term merely means to give charitable support, as in the person who sponsors someone else to swim a hundred metres or cycle a thousand kilometres. On the other hand, it can also mean the act of supporting another organisation in return for recognition: the best example of this meaning is the Premiership football teams who display their sponsors' logos over television sets all over the globe. The sponsors of charities may be less visible, but the principle is the same: the sponsor is being rewarded for its support; the charity is giving recognition of that support.

Charities and their sponsors need to consider the effects of the Charities Act 1992 on their arrangements (see 'Licences and Charity Law' above). A commercial sponsor may fall within the definition of a 'commercial participator' (see above). Whether or not the sponsor is a 'commercial participator' will depend upon whether or not a sponsorship payment amounts to the 'proceeds ... of a promotional venture'. Whether a sponsorship payment is a proceed is a difficult question to answer: it will depend upon the different facts of different arrangements. However, if the sponsor requests that the charity agree to the sponsor advertising their support on the sponsor's goods (e.g. 'XYZ Corporation is proud to announce that it has given £100,000 to ABC Charity'), then this will certainly make the sponsor a commercial participator.

This will also constitute a licence by ABC Charity to XYZ Corporation of its name, and ABC should consider the points made above about licensing.

# Charity law

Quite apart from the impact of the Charities Act 1992, charities that are considering entering into sponsorship deals also need to consider whether they have the appropriate power to do so. For those charities where the sponsorship underpins a primary-purpose activity it will be possible to argue that the charity is facilitating the achievement of its primary purpose. If that is not the case, what is the position? All charities have an express or implied power to carry on one-off fundraising activities, but a continuing sponsorship arrangement that does not underpin a primary purpose cannot be construed as a one-off event. It is a continuing activity that is not in fulfilment of a charity's primary purpose and therefore cannot be undertaken by the charity. To engage in any sponsorship where the turnover will exceed £50,000 or 25 per cent of the charity's income from all sources (whichever is the lower), the charity must establish a separate trading company instead. This in turn means that the charity should consider a number of key issues.

### Issues surrounding the establishment of trading companies

The first issue is whether the charity has the power in its constitution to establish a private company and to buy shares in it. Under the Trustee Act 2000 all charities that are unincorporated have wide powers to invest, subject to their duty to act in accordance with the standard duty of care. The Trustee Act 2000 does not apply to incorporated organisations. They should check their constitutions to ascertain if they have the power to invest in a private company. If it does not have this power, a charity will need to amend its constitution to enable it to invest in shares in a private company: this will require the consent of the Charity Commission. The charity will need to be able to justify its reasons for wanting to establish a trading company.

The second issue is the relationship between the charity and the trading company. It will be unlikely that a sponsorship arrangement will require working capital; but, if it does (e.g. because a joint marketing campaign needs to be financed), then the charity must abide by the Charity Commission's guidelines on investments in trading companies. Most such investment is by loan. Any loan must:

- not be interest free – interest should be charged at a reasonable and proper rate, based on the premise that the trustees are investing the charity's funds;

- be secured by a charge over the company's assets, even if these are only a stock of outdated Christmas cards;

- provide terms for its repayment – typically such loans are made repayable on demand.

Finally, there should be a contract between the trading company and the charity, setting out in detail their relationship and covering in particular such topics as:

- the price to be paid by the trading company for the use of the charity's assets (e.g. staff, office premises, databases, etc), normally calculated on an apportionment basis and invoiced monthly or quarterly in arrears;

- a non-exclusive licence from the charity to the trading company of the charity's name and logo, to enable the trading company to enter into licensing arrangements (see below).

The charges that are made by the charity to the trading company must be calculated on an arms-length basis; the charity must not provide the trading company with the right to use its assets at less than market value, as this could jeopardise the donation by the trading company to the charity of its profits under Gift Aid, as those donations must not be tainted by the suggestion of the donor receiving any benefit in return.

# VAT

Sponsorship payments will attract VAT, unless they are paid as part of a one-off fundraising event. For most corporate sponsors, this is not a problem: the charity (or its trading company) will render a VAT invoice for the amount of the sponsorship. The sponsor will in most cases have no problem with this, as it is able to recover any input VAT. However, problems do arise where the sponsor carries on exempt supplies (e.g. financial services or insurance). In these cases, they cannot recover the VAT, so for them VAT is an additional expense, which they will be reluctant to incur. Faced with this problem, many sponsors who carry out exempt supplies insist on the charity bearing the VAT. If a sponsorship of £10,000 is treated as VAT inclusive, and the charity has to account for the VAT out of the £10,000, it loses VAT of 17.5 per cent on £8,510, i.e. £1,490 (£8,510 grossed up at 17.5 per cent = £10,000).

To respond to this, some charities have arranged the relationship as follows:

- The charity and the sponsor agree to divide the sponsorship into two. One payment will be for the advertising services to be granted to the sponsor by the charity. The split must be fair and proper and capable of being justified to Customs and Excise. That payment will attract VAT and, for the reasons set out below, will be paid to the charity's trading company.

- The other payment will be a gift, to be paid to the charity and to be made under Gift Aid.

There should be two documents to regulate this:

- An agreement between the trading company and the sponsor to deal with the sponsorship, the licence of the sponsor's trademark and name to the trading company, and the services to be rendered to the sponsor;

- A deed between the sponsor and the charity committing the sponsor to make the agreed donation. If the gift is made up front, so that the charity has it at the outset, a deed will be unnecessary; but many of these arrangements provide for the gift to be paid in stages. If so, the commitment must be by deed, as otherwise it is legally unenforceable. A mere promise to pay cannot be enforced unless the promise is made by deed.

Another variant may be suggested by those would-be sponsors who carry on VAT exempt supplies and who have their own charity, funded by donations from the sponsor (e.g. the XYZ Company Charitable Trust). It has been known for the sponsor to propose that, because of the VAT issues, the sponsorship payments should come as a form of charitable grant from the XYZ Company Charitable Trust. If the recipient charity ('ABC') merely receives the grant and gives a small acknowledgement in its annual report, there is no problem. But what if the XYZ Company Charitable Trust has the same corporate style as XYZ Company? And what if the XYZ Company Charitable Trust insists that its name and style appear on ABC's notepaper? In these circumstances, it seems clear that ABC is rendering advertising services to the XYZ Company Charitable Trust; consequently, VAT should be charged by ABC on the value of the 'grant'.

## Direct tax (corporation and income tax)

The rules relating to sponsorship income and direct tax are far from easy. In the usual sponsorship arrangements, so far as the sponsor is concerned the payment is a tax-deductible business expense. But the position is far more complicated from the charity's point of view. Before analysing the Inland Revenue rules, it is worth emphasising the point that corporation or income tax is only paid on profits, and it is unlikely that any event or activity that receives sponsorship will yield a surplus on the sponsorship income. Normally there are plenty of expenses to offset against the sponsorship income so as to ensure there is no surplus.

Charities are exempt from taxation on profits if:

- the profits are applied solely for the purposes of the charity and
- either (a) the trade is exercised in the course of the actual carrying out of a primary purpose of the charity (i.e. the main objects of the charity as set out in the charity's constitution) or (b) the work in connection with the trade is mainly carried out by beneficiaries of the charity (e.g. the sale of goods produced by disabled people in workshops).

Unfortunately for charities, the activity of providing advertising services to sponsors does not fall neatly into the categories of tax exempt trading. It is not a primary-purpose activity for a charity to provide advertising services in return for a fee.

The Inland Revenue draws a distinction between:

- sponsorship that underwrites or follows a primary purpose and
- sponsorship that is stand-alone trade.

In the case of sponsorship that follows a primary-purpose trade (e.g. support from a sponsor of a charitable theatre company), the Revenue accepts that any surplus that the charity obtains from the sponsorship deal is tax free, as it is part of the income derived by the charity from carrying on its primary purpose – in this case, operating a charitable theatre.

On the other hand, if the sponsorship does not underwrite a primary-purpose trade, the position is different. For example, a charity that is established to alleviate poverty in developing countries circulates information packs on development issues free of charge to schools. The costs are underwritten by XYZ Company, whose name and logo are given prominent display on the pack. If (and it is a major 'if') the charity makes a surplus on the arrangement, that surplus will be taxable as being income derived from carrying out a non-primary-purpose business of providing advertising services – unless the charity can show that the trading activity falls within two exemptions:

1   That the trade is ancillary to the fulfilment of its primary purpose (e.g. a bar in a charitable theatre). In this case provided the *turnover* from the trade is:

    – less than 10 per cent of the total turnover of the charity and

    – less than £50,000 per annum,

then any profits will be tax free.

2   That the trade is not ancillary but falls within the new exemption available from April 2000 to exempt profits of small trading and other fundraising activities carried on by charities. The relief will apply where the charity has a reasonable expectation that the turnover will be no greater than either:

    – £5,000 or

    – the lesser of £50,000 and 25 per cent of the charity's gross income.

Note that this applies to turnover and not profits.

### Examples

a)  A charity has a gross income of £150,000

The maximum turnover of non-primary-purpose trade under the exemption that can be put through the charity is $150 \times 25$ per cent = £37,500.

b)  A charity has a gross income of £2 million

The maximum turnover of non-primary-purpose trade it can put through the charity is £50,000.

What is worse, the Revenue also has the capacity to tax all the profits of a charity that derive from a mixed primary- and non-primary-purpose trade: in other words, by creating a surplus from sponsorship, a charity could expose its profits from primary-purpose activities to the risk of tax too! This means that charities engaging in sponsorship deals that do not underwrite a primary-purpose trading activity and which fall outside the two exemptions should consider carefully whether that activity should be put through a trading company.

# Conclusion

As this chapter shows, different types of corporate fundraising strategies can give rise to different legal and tax consequences, some of them complicated. Charities entering into such arrangements need to understand all the detail involved and subject that detail to proper legal and tax analysis in order to ensure that the arrangements are structured appropriately to minimise the risks. Failure to do this could mean that the charity suffers unnecessary taxation. If that is the case, trustees of a charity could be taken to have acted in breach of their trust and could be sued and ordered to pay the charity the amount that the charity had lost, out of their own pockets, if the case against them were proven. This may sound fanciful, but the Charity Commission is on record as stating that trustees who allow their charities to incur unnecessary tax bills could themselves be personally liable for any loss so suffered. The only way to ensure that arrangements are structured in the most tax-efficient manner is to understand the details from the outset and, if appropriate, take specialist professional advice.

# Example of a corporate fundraising strategy

**Valerie Morton**

1   A reference to the organisation's overall fundraising strategy, indicating how corporate fundraising fits into this

2   Research – summary of previous corporate fundraising activity, SWOT, PEST, competitor analysis

3   Strategic objectives

- Financial – target net contribution from corporate fundraising for year 1, year 3 and year 5.

- How target is to be achieved in terms of gross income, direct costs and net contribution.

- Operational – e.g. to achieve x Charity of the Year collaborations, y cause-related marketing initiatives and z logo-licensing agreements (including timescale within which these targets are seen).

- Qualitative – e.g. to enhance our reputation with major companies that have their own occupational health departments to the point where our services are considered relevant to their occupational health programmes.

4   Regional strategy (if appropriate)
Review possible options, as between a national approach, an exclusive focus on London, a particular regional bias, a single-region pilot test, followed by a national roll-out, etc. End by defining priorities.

5   Industrial sector strategy
Review options with all major industrial sectors, e.g. engineering, manufacturing, financial services, sport, tourism, retailing, etc. Define no-go areas and priority areas.

6   Type of partnership
Review options as between seeking cash support, employee fundraising, CRM, gifts in kind, personnel secondments, etc. Define priorities.

7   Fundraising focus
Review options on which part of your charity's operations you want corporate fundraising to support, e.g. core funding, development projects, building work, special events sponsorship, etc. Define priorities.

8   Resourcing the strategy

- Internal resource
Outline recruitment and training needs to deliver the strategy. Consider the implications for office accommodation, IT systems, etc. Include implications on other departments in the organisation, which might need to gear up their resource to service the corporate fundraising strategy, in particular PR resource.

- External resource
Review the possible need for contracting the services of marketing agencies, consultants, etc in order to implement the strategy.

9   Time plan
Indicate critical timings on major parts of the strategic plan.

10  Five-year financial model
Make clear that the tabulated figures supplied here are not a year-by-year forecast of financial out-turn (these forecasts will appear as part of each year's budget-setting routine) but an indication of likely movements in income and expenditure that would result from successful implementation of the corporate fundraising strategic plan.
Also indicate which costs should be regarded as investment costs, as distinct from annually recurring costs.
Add an 'opportunity contingency' element to each year's projected figures.

# Corporate sources, with web sites

**Chris Carnie**

| Name | Source | Description |
| --- | --- | --- |
| The Guide to UK Company Giving | Directory of Social Change, www.dsc.org.uk | Basic company guide. |
| Advertisers Annual: the blue book | Hollis Directories Ltd, annual, www.hollis-pr.com | Advertising agencies, advertisers, brand names. |
| BRAD | Emap Business Communication, www.intellagencia.com | Advertising agencies, advertisers, brand names. Searchable on their web site 'BRADnet'. |
| Britain's Top Privately Owned Companies | Jordans Publishing Ltd, www.jordans.co.uk | Unquoted UK companies with rankings by turnover. |
| Business Age | Priori Publishing Ltd, monthly, www.businessage-online.com | People in business with a focus on the UK. |
| Business and Environmental Groups | Directory of Social Change, www.dsc.org.uk | |
| Carol | Carol Ltd, www.carol.co.uk | Annual reports for European, companies across the world. |
| CD-ROM Company Giving Guide | Directory of Social Change, www.dsc.org.uk | Information on over 500 UK companies. Search by geographic location, area of benefit, industry sector, pre-tax profit, associated brand name, directors' names, and subsidiary companies' names. |
| Chambers Directory | Chambers and Partners, annual, www.chambersandpartners.com | Web site with solicitors and barristers for the UK. Lists more than 3,500 solicitors, with regional reviews and ranking by size. |
| Companies House | Companies House, www.companies-house.gov.uk/ | Filings on paper, microfiche and computer on UK companies. The original source of UK company information. |
| Corporate Citizen | Directory of Social Change, three times per year, www.dsc.org.uk | Comments and case studies on corporate philanthropy in the UK. |
| D&B MarketPlace UK | Dun & Bradstreet, www.dnb.com | CD-ROM directory of UK companies. |

| Name | Source | Description |
|---|---|---|
| *DASH* | Dun & Bradstreet, quarterly, www.dnb.com | CD-ROM of major shareholders, directors of UK companies. Shows share issue prices. Can be searched geographically and by name. |
| *Directory of Directors* | Bowker Saur, annual, www.bowker-saur.co.uk | UK directors and their board appointments. Includes biographic information. |
| *Economist* | The Economist Group, www.economist.com | Magazine covering economics and business issues. |
| *EIRIS* | Ethical Investment Research Service, www.eiris.org | EIRIS was set up in 1983 with the help of churches and charities that had investments and needed a research organisation to help them put their principles into practice. EIRIS provides independent research into corporate behaviour and helps charities and other investors identify appropriate companies. |
| *Financial Times* | Financial Times, www.ft.com/ | UK's leading financial newspaper. Searchable archives online. Includes online ordering of UK plc annual reports. |
| *Hollis UK Press and Public Relations Annual* | Hollis Directories Ltd, annual, www.hollis-pr.com | Directory of PR consultancies and people. |
| *Hoover's Online* | Hoovers, www.hoovers.com | Corporate financial information including director information for companies around the world, with a US bias. |
| *ICC Information Ltd* | ICC Information Ltd, www.icc.co.uk | A supplier of online and CD-ROM information about UK and international companies. Their 'Juniper' online service includes 5.3 million UK limited companies, sole traders and partnerships, and over 8 million directorships. |
| *Incomes Data Services* | Incomes Data Services, www.incomesdata.co.uk/ | Information and reports about salaries for directors and others. |
| *Institute of Chartered Accountants in England and Wales: Directory of Firms* | Macmillan Press Ltd, annual, www.macmillan.co.uk | Directory of accountancy firms. |
| *Kelly's* | Reed Business Information, www.reedinfo.co.uk | Directory of companies by postal address. Online version available. |
| *Key British Enterprises* | Dun & Bradstreet, www.dnb.com | Available as book and as CD-ROM; covers the UK's largest 50,000 businesses by turnover. CD-ROM covering up to 200,000 businesses is updated quarterly. |

| Name | Source | Description |
|---|---|---|
| *Kompass* | Reed Information Services, www.kompassregister.co.uk | Brand name for a variety of business directories based on listings of products. Reed publish various Kompass directories including Kompass CD Plus, Kompass Online, UK Kompass Resiter Products and Services and Company Information (vols 1&2) and UK Kompass Regional Sales. |
| *Lahmann Communcations Company Guide* | HS Financial Publishing, quarterly, www.hsfinancial.com | Financials and facts about 2,300 UK stockmarket companies. |
| LexisNexis | www.lexisnexis.com | Website providing news, legal and business information, and public records. |
| *Major UK Companies Handbook* | Primark Extel, part of Thomson Financial, twice yearly, www.primark.com | Financial information on 850 quoted UK companies including directors, registered addresses. |
| *Marketing Week* | Marketing Week, weekly, www.mad.co.uk | Magazine for marketing management. |
| *PricewaterhouseCoopers Corporate Register* | HS Financial Publishing, quarterly, www.hsfinancial.com | Financials, directors and advisers of UK stockmarket companies. Includes biographic information and shareholdings. Also available as CD-ROM. |
| *Reed Business Information* | Reed Information Services, www.reedinfo.co.uk | Information from *Kompass*, *Kelly's Directory*, *Dial Industry* and *Directory of Directors*. 1.3m companies world-wide are profiled, of which 200,000 are in the UK. In addition all 1.5m companies from Companies House are detailed. |
| *Smaller UK Companies Handbook* | Financial Times Information (Extel Financial), annual, www.info.ft.com | Financial information on 1,500 smaller quoted UK companies. |
| *Sponsorship & Donations Yearbook* | Hollis Directories Ltd, annual, www.hollis-pr.com | Sponsors, agencies, sponsor-seeking organisations, sponsor policies. |
| *Who Owns Whom* | Dun & Bradstreet, www.dnb.com | Two-volume directory showing companies and their subsidiaries. Available as CD-ROM. |

# About the Directory of Social Change

The Directory of Social Change (DSC) is an independent voice for positive social change, set up in 1975 to help voluntary organisations become more effective. It does this by providing practical, challenging and affordable information and training to meet the current, emerging and future needs of the sector.

DSC's main activities include:

- researching and publishing reference guides and handbooks;
- providing practical training courses;
- running conferences and briefing sessions;
- organising Charityfair, the biggest annual form for the sector;
- encouraging voluntary groups to network and share information;
- campaigning to promote the interests of the voluntary sector as a whole.

**The Directory of Social Change**

24 Stephenson Way
London
NW1 2DP

Federation House
Hope Street
Liverpool
L1 9BW

*Publications and subscriptions*
tel: 020 7209 5151
fax: 020 7391 4804

*Publicity*
tel: 020 7391 4900

*Research*
tel: 020 7391 4880
0151 708 0136

*Courses and conferences*
tel: 020 7209 4949
0151 708 0117

*Charityfair*
tel: 020 7209 4949
020 7209 1015 (exhibitors)

website: www.dsc.org.uk
e-mail: books@dsc.org.uk

# Other publications from the Directory of Social Change

All the following titles are published by the Directory of Social Change, unless otherwise stated, and are available from:

Publications Department
Directory of Social Change
24 Stephenson Way
London
NW1 2DP

Call 020 7209 5151 or e-mail books@dsc.org.uk for more details and for a free publications list, which can also be viewed at the DSC website (www.dsc.org.uk).

Prices were correct at the time of going to press but may be subject to change.

## The fundraising series
**Published in association with CAF and the Institute of Fundraising.**

### Community Fundraising

*Edited by Harry Brown*

Volunteer networks are a key resource for fundraising, but are often not appreciated as they should be. This new title demonstrates how to make the most of your volunteers. It covers:

- what community fundraising is
- why people volunteer, the value of volunteers and staff attitudes to volunteers
- the recruitment, retention and development of volunteers
- the management of staff working with volunteers
- case studies from a range of different types of charities – and what can be learned from these.

192 pages, 1st edition, 2002
ISBN 1 900360 98 5 £19.95

### Fundraising Strategy

*Redmond Mullin*

The key to successful fundraising is rigorous strategic planning and this influential title has become essential reading for all serious fundraisers, as a background to the whole series. The second edition draws on some more recent examples, such as the NSPCC Full Stop campaign, to further clarify the principles and process of strategy and demonstrate its place in fundraising campaigns. The book:

- discusses the concept of strategy and its relevance to not-for-profit bodies
- outlines the planning process for designing and implementing the strategy
- provides case studies of different strategies in different types and sizes of funding programmes
- has been fully updated to take into account important changes in areas such as the tax regime and the National Lottery.

c.152 pages, 2nd edition, available August 2002

ISBN 1 903991 22 6 c.£19.95

### Legacy Fundraising
### The Art of Seeking Bequests

*Edited by Sebastian Wilberforce*

This unique guide to one of the most important sources of revenue for charities has been revised and updated to include new material on telephone fundraising, forecasting income, and profiling. It also contains the full text of the new Institute of Fundraising Code of Practice on legacy fundraising. Contributions from a range of experts in the field cover both strategy and techniques, and are complemented by perspectives from donors and their families. The breadth of coverage and accessible style ensure that, whether you are an established legacy fundraiser or new to the field, this book is a must.

224 pages, 2nd edition, 2001

ISBN 1 900360 93 4 £19.95

### Fundraising Databases

*Peter Flory*

Computerised databases are an essential tool for fundraising, but fundraisers often lack the technical background to help them choose a suitable database and use it effectively. This new book provides a clear framework for making and implementing such decisions. It explains what a database is and how it works, before going on to examine:

- why fundraisers need a database
- the functions of a fundraising database
- future trends

Case studies from a range of charities are used throughout to illustrate the points made.

160 pages, 1st edition, 2001

ISBN 1 900360 91 8 £19.95

### Trust Fundraising

*Edited by Anthony Clay*

This book outlines a variety of approaches to trusts that will save trustees' time and ensure greater success for fundraising by:

- emphasising the importance of research and maintaining records;
- demonstrating the value of using contacts and a personal approach;
- reinforcing the need for detailed planning of a strategy;
- showing how to make an approach to trusts, and how not to;
- stressing the importance of continued contact with a trust.

152 pages, 1st edition, 1999

ISBN 1 85934 069 5 £19.95

# Other titles from DSC

### The Complete Fundraising Handbook

*Nina Botting & Michael Norton*

Published in association with the Institute of Fundraising

For the new edition of this ever-popular title, the information has been completely updated and also reorganised, making it even easier to use. It is now divided into three parts, covering:

- fundraising principles and strategies
- sources of fundraising – including individual donors, grant-making trusts, companies, central and local government
- fundraising techniques – from house-to-house collections and challenge events, to direct mail and capital appeals.

Illustrated with case studies throughout, the book provides a wealth of practical advice on every aspect of fundraising for charity.

368 pages, 4th edition, 2001

ISBN 1 900360 84 5 £16.95

## Finding Company Sponsors For Good Causes

*Chris Wells*

Long-term sponsorship deals can benefit your organisation for more than one-off corporate donations. This book will help fundraisers secure company sponsorship with advice on how to:

- approach the potential sponsor
- convince them that you are a credible commercial partner
- target your proposal and set a sponsorship fee
- negotiate a deal and manage the project

96 pages, 1st edition, 2000

ISBN 1 900360 37 3 £9.95

## The Grant-Making Trusts CD-ROM

*Software development by Funderfinder*

Published in association with CAF

This CD-ROM combines the trusts databases of the Directory of Social Change and the Charities Aid Foundation to provide the most comprehensive and up-to-date information ever on grant-making trusts. The improved search facilities ensure fast, easy and effective searching across the whole database.

*Contents*

- Around 4,000 trusts as listed in the *Directory of Grant Making Trusts 2001–2002*, the three *Guides to Major Trusts 2001/2002 and 2002/2003*, and the four *Guides to Local Trusts 2002/2003*
- Full commentary from DSC guide displayed if available
- DGMT entry displayed for smaller trusts where full commentary is unavailable.

*Search facilities*

- Powerful combined search by geographical area, type of activity and type of beneficiary
- Search by name of trust, location, type of grant or trustee (improved for 2002)

- Search by key word

  *Software*

- PC format only
- Runs on Windows 95 and above
- Network capability
- 'Getting started' tutorial
- Hyperlinks to trust websites or e-mail
- Facility to bookmark selected trusts, add your own notes, print individual entries and tag for printing or export.

  Single CD-ROM, 2nd edition 2002

  ISBN 1 903991 12 9 £110 + VAT = £129.25

  £80 + VAT = £94 for existing users

### Website: trustfunding.org.uk

www.trustfunding.org.uk contains all the same data as the Grant-making Trusts CD-ROM, but will be regularly updated throughout the year.

- Search on geographical area, type of activity or type of beneficiary; by name of trust, name of trustee, type of grant, or location; key word search.
- Browser requirements: Internet Explorer version 4 and above or Netscape version 4 and above.
- Hyperlinks to trust websites or e-mail.
- Facility to print individual trust records and tag contact and address details for export.

  *Annual subscription*

  Charities and voluntary organisations: £110 + VAT = £129.25

  Statutory and commercial organisations: £150 + VAT = £176.25

  Register using a user name and password of your choice. You can then log on to the site as often as you wish for the duration of your subscription

# About CAF

CAF, Charities Aid Foundation, is a registered charity with a unique mission – to increase the substance of charity in the UK and overseas. It provides services that are both charitable and financial which help donors make the most of their giving and charities make the most of their resources.

As an integral part of its activities, CAF works to raise standards of management in voluntary organisations. This includes the making of grants by its own Grants Council, sponsorship of the Charity Annual Report and Accounts Awards, seminars, training courses and the Charities Annual Conference, the largest regular gathering of key people from within the voluntary sector. In addition, Charitynet (www.charitynet.org) is now established as the leading Internet site on voluntary action.

For decades, CAF has led the way in developing tax effective services to donors, and these are now used by more than 250,000 individuals and 2,000 of the UK's leading companies, between them giving £150 million each year to charity. Many are also using CAF's CharityCard, the world's first debit card designed exclusively for charitable giving. CAF's unique range of investment and administration services for charities includes the CafCash High Interest Cheque Account, two common investment funds for longer-term investment and a full appeals and subscription management service.

CAF's activities are not limited to the UK, however. Increasingly, CAF is looking to apply the same principles and develop similar services internationally, in its drive to increase the substance of charity across the world. CAF has offices and sister organisations in the United States, Bulgaria, South Africa, Russia, India and Brussels.

CAF Research is a leading source of information and research on the voluntary sector's income and resources. Its annual publication, *Dimensions of the Voluntary Sector*, provides year-on-year updates and its Research Report series covers a wide range of topics, including costs benchmarking, partnership resources, and trust and company funding. More details on research and publications may be found on www.CAFonline.org/research

For more information about CAF, please visit www.CAFonline.org/

# About the Institute of Fundraising

The Institute of Fundraising is the only organisation that exists to represent and support the professional interests of fundraisers at all levels. The Institute of Fundraising welcomes membership applications from all those working in a fundraising role or consultancy practice – from those new to the profession to those with many years' experience.

The benefits to be gained are available to all. As a professional body, the Institute of Fundraising assists its members at every stage and in every facet of their professional development. It provides opportunities for continuing professional education, a forum for discussion on issues of common concern, a source of information and a point of contact with other professionals.

The Institute of Fundraising Certificate of Membership is evidence of the holder's commitment to the Codes and the professional standards set by the Institute. Since membership is individual, it is fully transferable if you change your job. In liaison with other umbrella groups, the Institute of Fundraising also represents members' interests to charities, government, the media and to the public.

The Institute of Fundraising is supported financially by many charities who recognise the importance and needs of the organisation, having become affiliates of its Charitable Trust. Fundraising staff of these affiliated charities enjoy reduced subscription fees. Through its members, the Institute of Fundraising liaises worldwide with allied organisations, such as the National Society of Fundraising Executives in the USA and the Australian Institute of Fundraising, and is represented on the World Fundraising Council.

The Institute of Fundraising aims, through its Trust, to further knowledge, skills and effectiveness in the field of fundraising. It serves the interests of its members, the professional fundraisers, and through them, the interests of charitable bodies and donors. The Institute of Fundraising aims to set and develop standards of fundraising practice which encompass:

- growth in the funds and resources available for charitable expenditure;
- thorough knowledge of proven fundraising techniques;
- new fundraising opportunities;
- cost effectiveness;
- strict adherence to the law;
- accountability.

# Institute of Fundraising Codes of Practice, Guidance Notes, and the Charity Donors' Rights Charter

The Institute of Fundraising Codes of Practice and Guidance Notes aim to act as a guide to best practice for fundraisers, and as a benchmark against which the public can measure fundraising practice. They cover a wide variety of issues and aim to address both practical and ethical concerns.

The Codes are drawn up by working parties composed of representatives of the various interested constituents in a particular field, and undergo an extensive consultation process through the charities affiliated to the Institute of Fundraising, regulators and government.

As new areas of interest are identified, so new Codes are drafted, often at the rate of two or three each year, under the supervision of the Institute of Fundraising Standards Committee. Both Charity Commission and Home Office are represented on this committee and play a major role in the development of any new work.

The Codes are endorsed and observed by fundraising organisations throughout the UK. They are recognised as demonstrating the commitment of the voluntary sector to the promotion of best practice.

The Charity Donors' Rights Charter has been developed as a compact between fundraisers and the supporters of the organisations for which they work. It aims to address the expectations that a supporter has of the organisation they give to, and to articulate the commitment the sector makes to them.

## Codes of Practice

Charity Challenge Events
UK Charity Challenge Events
Fundraising in Schools
House to House Collections
Telephone Recruitment of Collectors
Personal Solicitation of Committed Gifts
Legacy Fundraising
Outbound Telephone Support

Payroll Giving
Reciprocal Charity Mailings

## Guidance Notes

The Acceptance and Refusal of Donations
Data Protection Act 1998
The Management of Static Collection Boxes
The Use of Chain Letters as a Fundraising Technique
UK Charity Challenge Events

## New Codes for 2001

Raffles and Lotteries
Fundraising on the Internet

Copies of the Codes of Practice, Guidance Notes and Charity Donors' Rights Charter may be obtained from the Institute of Fundraising at:

Institute of Fundraising
5th Floor
Market Towers
1 Nine Elms Lane
London SW8 5NQ
Tel: 020 7627 3436

Or from:
enquiries@institute-of-fundraising.org.uk

# Index